Copyright © 2011 Chris Green and Liam Heneghan

All rights reserved. No part of this book may be reproduced in any form or by any electronic or mechanical means, including information storage and retrieval systems, without permission in writing from the publisher, except for review.

Published by
DePaul University Humanities Center
DePaul Poetry Institute
DePaul University Institute for Nature & Culture

Chicago, Illinois

First edition
10 9 8 7 6 5 4 3 2 1

ISBN 13: 978-06154252-9-0
Library of Congress Control Number: 2010941862

Printed in the United States of America
Set in Hoefler Text

Brute Neighbors

Urban Nature Poetry,
Prose & Photography

EDITED BY CHRIS GREEN & LIAM HENEGHAN

BRUTE NEIGHBORS

urban nature poetry, prose and photography

DePAUL HUMANITIES CENTER

DePAUL UNIVERSITY HUMANITIES CENTER
DePAUL POETRY INSTITUTE
DePAUL UNIVERSITY INSTITUTE FOR NATURE & CULTURE

CHICAGO, ILLINOIS

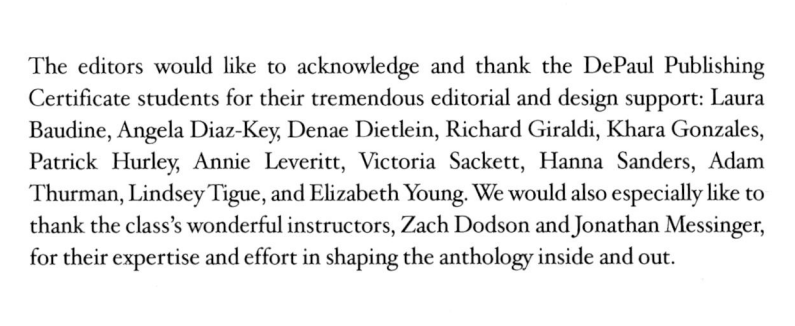

The editors would like to acknowledge and thank the DePaul Publishing Certificate students for their tremendous editorial and design support: Laura Baudine, Angela Diaz-Key, Denae Dietlein, Richard Giraldi, Khara Gonzales, Patrick Hurley, Annie Leveritt, Victoria Sackett, Hanna Sanders, Adam Thurman, Lindsey Tigue, and Elizabeth Young. We would also especially like to thank the class's wonderful instructors, Zach Dodson and Jonathan Messinger, for their expertise and effort in shaping the anthology inside and out.

The editors would also like to thank Anna Vaughn Clissold and Jonathan Gross at DePaul's Humanities Center for their intelligent direction and kind support.

For Lexa, Callie and Lydie, always. −*CG*

&

For Vassia, who decades later still confirms the irreducibility of life's finest things. −*LJH*

Table of Contents

PREFACE 17

POEMS

Ravenswood	Stuart Dybek	23
Hungry	David Baker	24
The House in Plano	Susan Hahn	25
The Affect of Elms	Reginald Gibbons	27
Summer Surprised Us	Edward Hirsch	28
DED (Dutch Elm Disease)	Don Share	30
High Holidays	Don Share	31
Beggar Girl	Billy Lombardo	32
Container Garden	Rachel Jamison Webster	33
Bound Boundless	Deborah Nodler Rosen	34
In This Hour	Ralph Mills	35
Moon's/Flying	Ralph Mills	36
A Slow	Ralph Mills	37
Torque	Maureen Seaton	38
construction	cin salach	39
Deer Sonnets	Chris Green	40
Lotus Garden	Patricia McMillen	42
Where the Window Begins	Margaret Brady	44
Tiny Moon Notebook	David Trinidad	45
Coyotes of Lakeshore Drive	Kristy Bowen	54
Birds of Paradise	Rachel Contreni Flynn	55
Ever since	Helen Degen Cohen	57
Rising for the Buddha	Dina Elenbogen	59
Chicago Harvest	Maureen Tolman Flannery	60
Missing Us	Mary Hawley	61

The Day is 7:03 AM, the Smoking Smart Car	Mike Puican	62
Small Boy	Marc Smith	63
Storm Lessons	Patricia Monaghan	66
July as a 1950's Sci-Fi movie	Susen James	67
Nocturnal	Alice George	68
This Is to Find Out about Something	Arielle Greenberg	70
Mechanical Foliage	James Shea	73
Once the magnolia has blossomed	Ed Roberson	74
Brumation	Kathleen Kirk	76
Blue Trees	Larry Janowski	77
The Fox	Richard Jones	78
Benched	E. Ethelbert Miller	79
In the Intersection, Jackson and State	Tony Trigilio	80
Wherever	Virginia Bell	81
One day	Cecilia Pinto	82
Night in a strange city	Julie Parson Nesbitt	83
Under the Full Crust Moon	Martha Modena Vertreace-Doody	84
Borders	Elise Paschen	86
Tree of Heaven	Barry Silesky	88
It Takes Particular Clicks	Christian Wiman	92
Subdivision Ghazal	Jan Bottiglieri	94
Unruly Urban Youth	Brenda Cardenas	95
What Garfield Park Kept Saying	Patricia Smith	96
Entering Strange Cities	Allan Johnston	98
Hawk Hour	Mark Turcotte	100
Windy City	Christina Pugh	101

PHOTOGRPAHY

Look at you	***Dolores Wilber***	103
"41° N, 87° W, (Chicago)"	***Mary Jane Duffy***	106
Predation	***Liam Heneghan***	108
EDEN/extracts	***Mark Curran***	109
Rogers Park	***Randall Honold***	113
Montrose Harbor	***Randall Honold***	114
Elston Avenue	***Randall Honold***	115

NONFICTION

17-Year Itch	Miles Harvey	116
Boy Eats World	Michele Morano	122
Plain Scared, or: There Is No Such Thing as Negative Space, the Art Teacher Said	S.L. Wisenberg	127
A City of Human-clams: a Plea for Environmental Immobility	Liam Heneghan	134
Nature Drawings	***Peter Karklins***	138
Archaic Nature	Sean Kirkland	141
Old Airs	Perry A. Zurn	146
A Garden in Eden	Barbara Willard	149

FICTION

Turf	Elizabeth Crane	152

ACKNOWLEDGMENTS   162
BIOS   166

NEIGHBORS

Preface

Brute Neighbors: Urban Nature and the redress of the arts.

Despite our brooding discontent, our lingering sense that our environing world is in decline, that the world around us is aflame with war, famine, disease, climate weirdness, that our cities are unlivable, that our economies are doomed to collapse, that we are brotherly and sisterly no more, that under our use and abuse, nature's web is frayed and weary; despite all of this, surely our best days should be ahead of us? We are, after all, a vernal species, freshly minted by evolutionary processes dating back no more than a couple of hundred-thousand years. If a species typically sticks around a million years, by simple calculation we have run less than a quarter of our course. Can we really have squandered all of our chances so very soon? In this volume we ask, paraphrasing poet Seamus Heaney, if poets, artists, creative writers, philosophers, and photographers can help *redress* the problems that beset us. Artists who live where the flames rise highest, that is in cities — seemingly the very epicenter of our crises — cannot necessarily be appealed to for succor in tough times, good art after all may do very little. But by the reckless blaze of good art, surely we can see the new terrain in all its ambiguity and complexity, and re-envision the task ahead in a more hopeful way than we have become used to.

Our natural proclivities equip us for debacle and solution in seemingly equal measure. Primates, such as we are, are characterized by generalized natures; there is little distinctive about all of us other than our lack of distinction. Said another way, we have evolutionary suppleness — a commitment to innovation. We humans, for instance, have no specialized defense mechanisms — we exude no toxic or noisome chemicals, our teeth may gnash but they do not assail, we have no carapace to shield our moist vulnerability. Biological features noteworthy about us are all extensions of our beastly condition: we are mobile, and we have brains swollen like ripe fruit atop erect bodies; clever apes that we are, we have perfected the manipulation of the surrounding world in a manner that extends our reach beyond bodily limitations — technology, another extension of primate innovation, is our ecology. For ninety-nine percent of our history we exclusively gathered, and occasionally hunted, and our numbers were modest; we lived within the confines of local ecological systems. Though perennially extending our range, pullulating out from our African home-range to encompass much of the inhabitable earth, we have generally been more constrained by nature than we were a strain on nature. A mere geological moment ago, everything changed. Ten thousand years ago we became dramatically less mobile; we cultivated and accumulated rather than collected; we domesticated plants and animals; and indeed we ultimately domesticated ourselves. The reverberations of this agricultural revolution, this domestication revolution, are still omnipresent. Anthropologists inform us that civilization and its accoutrements: permanent architecture, metallurgy, writing, villages, towns and cities, are aftershocks of the agricultural revolution.

About one year ago, a decided marker in the quarter-million-year gestation of this species was reached. Our primate tendencies of mobility, braininess, dexterousness, and suppleness, characteristics that had served us handsomely on the savannas of the world had resulted in the completion of the following colossal transition: we had now become an urban species. More than fifty per cent of the world's population now lives in cities!

Evolutionary biologists instruct us that if the evolutionary unfurling of any species is replayed, a different outcome would emerge. But in this particular incarnation, one primate, equipped by nature to change the rules, reorganized its behavioral routines and settled down in dense, sedentary communities supported by the cultivation of plants and animals in the surrounding terrain. Even when one regards the transition to *Homo metropolis* as a natural outgrowth of human evolutionary possibility, that is, part of the very "self-expression" of nature, it is clear that the boundaries of the cities are typically regarded as a threshold of nature: beyond the city limits is nature in the raw, nature as the really real; within the fleshpots of the city is the domain of culture. In the great Indian epics, the Rāmāyana and the Mahabharata, the heroes are exiled from the city into a wilderness of forest where danger and adventure lurk. The epic Gilgamesh too navigates the tension of the city and the wild. World literature repeatedly confirms what city dwellers intuit, nature has been left behind. Of this threshold, Yevgeny Zamyatin, author of the science-fiction classic *We,* says: "...between me and the wild green ocean was the glass of the Wall. Oh, great, divinely bounding wisdom of walls and barriers! They are perhaps, the greatest of man's inventions. Man ceased to be a wild animal only when he built the first wall. Man ceased to be a savage only when we had built the Green Wall, when we had isolated our perfect mechanical world from the irrational, hideous world of trees, birds, animals..." And yet, and yet...can it really be true, that nature surrounds and culture cocoons, that the really real is always somewhere we are not? Are we not born, do we not live, do we not lie down to die in cities; do we not eat and shit and fuck in cities? Do we not breathe in oxygen, that delicious excretion of plants in order to tend the little personal furnace in our own secret physiological core; do we not burble carbon dioxide when we light the taper of our ingesta? Are we not connected to the vast wheels of oxygen, carbon, nitrogen, phosphorus and sulfur cycling? Do plants not flourish in the interstices between our buildings? Do animals not know the night, use the night for their own private rummagings? "And for all this," to speak with Hopkins, "nature is never spent," not even in the vast metropoli of the world. All this, and more than this, on this side of the Green Wall?

In one of the foundational gestures of American environmental action, Henry David Thoreau walked out of town: "It is hard for me to believe," he informs us, "that I shall find fair landscapes or sufficient wildness and freedom behind the eastern horizon. I am not excited by the prospect of a walk thither; but I believe that the forest which I see in the western horizon stretches uninterruptedly toward the setting sun, and there are no towns nor cities in it of enough consequence to disturb me." The wildness towards which Thoreau sauntered is the territory that subsequently and overwhelmingly attracted the attention of the nascent environmental movement and the sciences that ultimately supported it. Although wilderness has not been an exclusive preoccupation of ecologists and conservationists in the last century, the attraction of the pristine, the unmanaged, the spatially immense, and the wild can be traced through the development of both ecological theory and conservation practice.

There is now a recognition that this imbalance in ecology needs to be redressed, and a variety of well-funded projects are underway to provide a firm theoretical and empirical basis for urban ecology. The importance of this reconfiguration in ecology is not just that it complements and challenges the discipline as a whole, but that it also provides an opportunity to calibrate theory developed in areas of lower human impact for its application in areas of high human density where the designation of land use is more highly variegated.

In return, a rigorously conceived urban ecology where the ecosystem and the social system are conjoined in a new urban manner may radicalize (and unify) ecology. From this new perspective, wilderness may be seen as a special case, rather than the foundational case, against which all is compared and deemed, usually, to have failed. This view of wilderness would remain intellectually generous to the wild, but would profoundly reorient our views. A scientific evaluation of nature in cities may facilitate a reevaluation of nature everywhere.

Excitement over this revolutionary turn in ecology — a sort of Copernican turn, where the perspectives that seemed least profitable, that is, the urban perspective, has become a cornerstone for a new ecology, led the editors of this volume to wonder whether there were similar revolutionary stirrings occurring in metropolitan arts. Unlike ecological thinkers, poets and artists, even when sharply criticized by Plato, have as often as not been urban in sensibility and in inspirations. For every daffodi—loving Wordsworth in the world's wind-swept places, there has been a body-loving Cavafy cavorting in an urban den. We therefore asked poets, photographers, essayists, and philosophers to respond to the theme of nature in the city. Of course, one assumes nature is important, but we wanted to see how artists are interacting *with* nature, or how they were seeing all of us interacting *in* nature. Math and science can go to work on nature as it is seen from the outside: nature as pattern and bold fact; but surely it takes an artist to respond to the patterns of our inside-nature; how our nature interacts with nature—our imagination, or the imagination. Only through art can certain relationships and emotions be expressed and understood. This is the sense in which we return to, and deploy, the notion of the "redress of poetry". Though the definitions of redress are legion, Heaney prefers an archaic term from hunting (itself very satisfactory for our purposes) where redress means "to bring back (the hounds or deer) to the proper course." If art lights up our inner-nature — shows us by its flare-lights where we are with/in/of nature right now — it can "redress" in the sense of allow us to find a course for the "breakaway of inner capacity". In this, we do not expect art to dampen our enthusiasm for the human project in its current urban manifestation; this art should not hinder. Rather we anticipate that it may allow us to encounter our fullest potential at a time when otherwise we might despair. Accordingly, the poems, stories, essays, and photographs in this anthology do not stand aloof — they are as bodies inclined forward in the wind, poems of the mass of the Midwest and its retired meadows and active capitalism, the unaccountable wildness of the most common streets.

LIAM HENEGHAN
CHRIS GREEN

Ravenswood

STUART DYBEK

Pigeons fold their wings and fade
into the gray facades of public places;
flags descend from banks, slips
floating to beds, while hips thrust

like those of lovers, as workers crank
through turnstiles, and waiting
for the Ravenswood express, at stations
level with the sky, they shield their eyes

with newspapers against a dying radiance:
that lull between trains, sunset's
stratified fire balanced on a gleaming spire.

Night doesn't *fall*, but rather
all the disregarded shadows of a day
flock like blackbirds, and suddenly rise.

Hungry

DAVID BAKER

This time the jay, fat as a boot, bluer
than sky gone blue now that the rain has
finished with us for a while, this loud jay
at the neck of the black walnut keeps cawing
I want, I want—but can't finish his clause.
Hard runoff has spread the driveway with seeds,
green talcum, the sex of things, packed
like plaster against shutters and tool boxes,
sides of the barn, while the force of water
pouring down from the stopped-up gullet
of gutter has drilled holes deep in the mud.
Yet the world of the neighborhood is still just
the world. So much, so much. Like the bulldog
next door, choking itself on a chain
to guard the yard of the one who starves it.

The House in Plano *SUSAN HAHN*

> *Nature may change; the house rests in geometric certitude*
> —Franz Schulze from *Mies van der Rohe, A Critical Biography*

It would be hard to hide in that house
without any cranny to curve into,
unlike here, where each corner provides
a shelter of brick, the view outside almost
a body's throw away. There, the spaces

between the planes and the pillars are glass,
the base five feet from the earth,
so it can ignore the river
and its occasional overflow. Nature

fluctuates while that rectangular box holds
firm against slick winds, leaden
snow and the sun on days it burns the rims
of the clouds. Here, in my nook—

a closet of reflection—sometimes only a siren
pulls me out to look onto the street
and even then I draw my shade
as when last week the ambulance shrieked:

lights and noise racing to the widow
in her bungalow across the road,
her small windows draped like closed eyes.
I don't know if she's dead
or alive, can only hope she'll reappear,
that I'll see her, when I glance out, glad

she's been given one more chance
over the forces that flood and push
us back further and finally
down, no wide-flange columns to secure
our floor above the ground.

The Affect of Elms   *REGINALD GIBBONS*

Across the narrow street from the old hotel that now
houses human damage temporarily—
deranged, debilitated, but up and around in their odd
postures, taking their meds, or maybe trading them—

is the little park, once a neighboring mansion's side yard,
where beautiful huge old elm trees, long in that place,
stand in a close group over the mown green lawn
watered and well kept by the city, their shapes expressive:

the affect of elms is of struggle upward and survival,
of strength—despite past grief (the bowed languorous arches)
and torment (limbs in the last stopped attitude of writhing)—

while under them wander the deformed and tentative
persons, accompanied by voices, counting their footsteps,
exhaling the very breath the trees breathe in.

Summer Surprised Us   EDWARD HIRSCH

These first days of summer are like the pail
of blueberries that we poured out together
into the iron sink in the basement—

a brightness unleashed and spilling over
with tiny bell-shaped flowers, the windows
opened and the shrubs overwhelming the house

like the memory of a forgotten country, Nature,
with its wandering migrations and changing borders,
its thickets, woodlands, bee-humming meadows...

These widening turquoise days in mid-June
remind me of slow drives through the country
with my parents, the roads spreading out

before us like the inexhaustible hours
of childhood itself, like the wildflowers
and fruit stands blooming along the highway,

the heat tingling on my skin that would
burn with the banked fires of adolescence
and the no less poignant ache of adulthood

on those long detours through the park
during the last rain-soaked nights of spring
and the first beach days of the season...

It's the leisurely amplitude of feeling
that rises out of these expanding afternoons,
the days facing outwards, the city taking notice

of itself after all these months, off-duty,
wearing short sleeve shirts and sleeveless dresses
the color of sunlight, the texture of morning.

It's the way we move towards each other
at night, tired, giddy after a day together
or a day apart, flush with newborn plans

for a holiday from daily life, in reality.
We are festive and free-floating. We are
poured out like a bucket of wild berries.

DED (Dutch Elm Disease) *DON SHARE*

The town came round and said
our tree must come down –
Like a bell without a clapper,
this yard without its elm.

High Holidays

DON SHARE

Rabbit fur and hair strewn through the lawns
        of the Midwest!
The famous feral parakeets of Chicago
        are chattering
With cold. I want to drown myself
        out with the roar
Of the greenish river that slices my city
        into two.
Nothing pertains, if that's the right word,
        to what I'm hearing:
Little kids singing Benjamin Britten's
        Ceremony of Carols or, if only
In my mind's ear, what I'm able to recall
        of the *Kol Nidre*:
Rushing over the notes, as if in an unearthly
        hurry to get someplace.

Beggar Girl

BILLY LOMBARDO

I don't know why the pigeons here make me think of you. Nor what whim moves them to flap and rise at once, makes them lift and soar and turn on sky dimes from one to another city ledge. They strike me as serious birds in small numbers. But up here, in hundreds, through these walls of glass, they stop you from reading, from doing small things with pens—make you see them as playful. Up here they are like doves or some other special bird. I didn't know what to do, today, with this thing I have for you. So I put it in the sky. I pretended this is what the pigeons were after—it was not some caprice after all. I pretended one of them saw it first and flapped its wings and then another saw it and then another. And then there were hundreds of them, chasing this faster, more serious, more playful thing than they.

Container Garden

RACHEL JAMISON WEBSTER

Talk stops in the self-conscious elevator.
The space is small and all the colors dim
referrals to steel, oil, coal—time-folds
of growth and decay, drilled out now
and burned against death into death.

Everyone's mute, gazing down
at their charcoal cuffs and tongueless shoes.
The prairie's gold robes, the sky's eye,
sunlight scratching the lake's wrinkled hide,
all have been dismissed as childish, too brash
for our palette of smog.

A drone and the doors slide open
to the rooftop of the future,
which is now. A hundred specimens
of grass kept separate in steel planters.
Grass that once was grass
and now is any caged thing.

Once a fish lent me her circular jaw
and I wore it as a crown. I stared out
from a diadem of teeth polished to a gleam.
I lifted it today from the tides of sleep,
brushed off sand and cleared the weeds
to recall a kingdom of beings who swam,
breathed, were eaten and ate with one mind.

Bound Boundless   *DEBORAH NODLER ROSEN*

"Death is so long I want to be happy there,
not a dark, damp coffin," he says, digging
out his forever home, caulking it with clay.

"Threads of platinum for my shroud,
cage me in glass. I want to see sun and stars,
breathing leaves, bright birds.

A pool at my feet for deer to drink;
at my head mounded grass teeming with life;
water and wood; sunflower and sage.

To lay all at ease in my own land,
my garden in my city."

In This Hour

RALPH MILLS

Air clings, moist as peeled fruit
from the afternoon heat—

I am watchful, dreaming.

A wind ripples ivy
outside the window,
spears of grass thrust
flame-tipped
even as the light goes.

Almost full, the moon
coats roofs a tarnished silver,
sharpens leaves
until they gleam.

River 'of the plains'
your wrist of moonswept brown water
curves into thought, distant
and thin.

In this hour
I wish for nothing
but to be filled with what I can see

and to walk to the half-open door
in the air ahead.

Moon's/Flying

RALPH MILLS

    moon's
            flying
at first dark,
                its
middle chipped out —
             beneath this up-
rising ailanthus
         blades of
    lily tuft clash
in the wind,
        impatiens blown,
red as coals,
        now leaves, aerial
leaflets, the wings of unknown
                            bodies
take flight—

A Slow   *RALPH MILLS*

   a slow
kind of
breeze
     parting leaf
from leaf
       this deliberation
letting yarrow
soar
   formally
like flat-topped
milky clouds
         while the air
mists
silvered grey
       & a window blinks
distantly
       opalescent as though
some-
one you remember
remembered
       you
  there
     & who maybe
waved—

Torque

MAUREEN SEATON

The day the funnels jockey like speeding UFOs along Bernard,
break from the blackened West like arms of a raging amoeba
to crash a path along Chicago's North Branch,
East on Foster, scissoring oaks, severing limbs
with the abandon and logic of a bowling team of gods, you
quit Choi's True Value and I gaze with longing
at photos of Wyoming, Tetons a cathedral of tranquility. It's
easy to die with your heart pounding in the sun parlor
surrounded by stained glass and flying buttresses.
Easy. when I run in circles from window to door,
back and forth with ontological questions tapping my skull
like—Which wall is a load-bearing wall or
Was this a warning or a watch—I know myself
puny and hysterical, craven and candescent, a star
imploding in the great order. I wish on myself.
I wish I wish I wish but everything is elemental—Lori
walking up Kimball without a clue, the old dog peeing
one block over, biting at hailstones. The cloud
passing by so quickly, the landlord says: What tornado?
And invites me to drink his booze. I'm obsessed with wind.
Green alien air, molecules torquing in the thunder, that leap
at the roof of the house like a crazed bionic, neither
friend nor foe, only bigger than everything that exists—
addiction, ad firms, computers, sex. Lori
turns the corner and the old dog rummages through recycling,
and all the photographs that were on my desk
that are now on the floor lie still as the dead. What's hard
is in the clearing that follows the noise like a thief,
that siphon of sweet adrenalin, all the wild horses, grazing.

construction   CIN SALACH

When the men leave there's a giant hole in the street which honestly doesn't surprise me. They tear it up then surround it with yellow "caution caution caution" tape which you know the wind is gonna blow off soon enough and then if you're not careful you could fall in or pop your tire or damage your suspension rods. It's true. A friend of mine had to get a whole new car because she drove into a hole in the street.

The workers leave one man behind on a folding chair holding a flip phone and sipping from a blue thermos. It's his job to watch the hole until the other men come back, or until the city sends further instruction, or until the hole miraculously fills itself back in. But really it's until someone calls him home for dinner and he can fold things up and drive away, his honest day's work done.

And who am I to make assumptions? Maybe he's going home to a sick mother. Maybe this is his first real job after months of unemployment. Maybe this is just the way streets get fixed in Chicago or sewers or whatever runs under these roads I think are so solid and apparently are not. Look at that hole. Drill a little ways down and it's all up for grabs. It's all open space and random construction and here I am driving around thinking it's all solid under there, but really it's air. I might as well be driving in the sky.

Deer Sonnets

CHRIS GREEN

Wayne Goldsberry killed a five-point whitetail deer with his bare hands after it crashed into his daughter's bedroom through a window. Goldsberry was able to break the buck's neck after a 40-minute struggle.
 —*Newsweek*

I kept the universe simple:
before I saw her, I saw a black or white answer.
She was a glimpse of summer lightning,
what I must be faithful to, a fidelity to fidelity.
It was not my own love but a counter-love,
an original response. She fed me apples.
I will never forget her deer eyes and her hands
like slipping fish in moonlight, her pale neck,
the pour of her hair. I never had a house,
and even as I came to her, she did not scare.
Little things made her glad—
she held my branches, nuzzled their velvet.
And she'd agreed to ride, despite my dread,
and disappear into destiny's trees.

He was short but fierce, a beard like a moose.
He sidled and circled. What was I to say?
I am a sexually mature hoofed mammal
with no money, but I make spectacular leaps.
His father-strength was indescribable,
no pretense or confusion—this was his house.
And me with my simple system of art,
of representation and defense—

each antler has its point—and my great speed.
He got my head turned, as if to kiss—
his anger pouring like a waterfall.
He would not let me change the world.
And he stumbled with me through her walls
and forced me to see—and that was all.

Lotus Garden

PATRICIA MCMILLEN

—for Sam

This morning the yoga instructor
strains to be heard
over sounds of a wood chipper
running full tilt in the alley
two floors down. When she says

feel your sitbones
against the ground

I imagine what is
below: wood planks,
I-beam, trapped air,
brick pilings, dead insects,
parked cars,

finally dirt.

* * *

The teacher says Relax

as hammering on sheet metal gives way
to the sound of a metal rake
being drawn across concrete. Lying flat,
my spine pressed to the mat,

thinking how much I love you,

I cry. Everything's
present:
bone branch leaf tendon
blood breath air

This is how it all happens

both inside and outside
simultaneously.

Where the Window Begins MARGARET BRADY

So the poet Robinson Jeffers (the hawk guy) says that "poetry is bound to concern itself chiefly with permanent things and the permanent aspects of life... Prose can discuss matters of the moment; poetry must deal with things that a reader two thousand years away could understand and be moved by." So, since this is a prose poem, I should probably talk about stuff going on right now, in the moment, as well as the big stuff – like the Big D. Right now, the birds are doing their morning rap. Sweet. A beat I can dance to. The sun is trying to poke through some serious nebulosity. My iced mocha caramel swirl Coolatta® is starting to kick in, and I'm trying to stay in the moment, for a moment. (Mocha this, latté that. Can you believe the industry that's developed around the innocent little coffee bean? Abso-fucking-lutely amazing.) Focus. See, that's my main problem. Trying to stay focused long enough to wrap a neuron or two around some idea. From one moment to the next. So, back to *this* moment, the sun is still dealing with "the low'ring element," as Milton referred to suck-ass skies. I'm putting my money on the sun. The birds are still doing their thing. Speaking of birds, a few days ago I found a wounded sparrow in front of a friend's place. Looks like he torpedoed right into her window. (Another good reason why you should never keep your windows *that* clean, for Chris'sake. How's a bird supposed to tell where the window begins and his life ends?) His neck looked broken. He bounced around on the ground like a little wind-up toy, trying to fly. My friend's husband wanted to whack the little guy right then and there – a "mercy" killing, he said. So we pulled an Anne Frank and hid the bird in the bushes until I could come back and take him to the animal shelter. Even in the back seat of my car, he kept trying to cut loose for the skies. I admire that. At the shelter, he flailed around, pretending that he was a bird and everything was cool. I've been meaning to call the shelter to find out what happened to the little guy. Was it the Big D, or is he in rehab? And what does that mean for the rest of us? Two thousand years from now, will we still be sipping Coolatta®s, waiting for the sun and trying to figure out these permanent aspects of life? Or will we have made it to the skies, through an open window?

Tiny Moon Notebook   *DAVID TRINIDAD*

—for Tony Trigilio

A perfect half
moon. Walking
Byron. Hot
breezy night.

*

Above the roof of
the building across
the street: a bright
gibbous moon in a
nest of silvery clouds.

*

Corner of Hollywood
and Glenwood.
Above trees: moon,
just about full, obscured
by small puffy clouds.
First hint of fall.

*

Full moon, moonlit-
clouds—through
trees.

*

Clouds moving
across the round
moon. The night
Jim died.

*

Walking down Clark
St. with Doug. The
moon, waning, against
a black backdrop,
above Alamo Shoes.

*

Leaving Jim's place
with Priscilla: a
gibbous moon, lightly
smeared, between
telephone wires.

*

Doug and I walking
out of Whole Foods in
Evanston: gibbous moon
on a clean blackboard.
Doug eating a cookie;
me, a Rice Krispie treat.

*

The moon, almost full,
glowing a little, but alone
in the sky. A yellow
leaf fell in front of me.

*

Radiant and
full, the moon,
alone in the
sky.

*

Walking Byron
(with Doug) on
Hollywood Ave.—
whiteness through
the trees.

*

Hollywood and Ridge:
waning gibbous,
out of focus.
Beneath it: a
bluish wisp.

*

Outside Ebenezer Church:
the moon, shy of
half, and fast-moving

gray streaks.

*

Glenwood and Hollywood.
Everything pointing up:
steeple of Edgewater Baptist
Church, trees—one stripped
clean, one hanging on to half
its yellow leaves. The tip
of the latter touching the sharp
point of the half moon.
It looked like a blade.

*

Half moon on its
back, quickly enveloped
by orangish-gray gauze,
through wind-tossed
trees.

*

Gibbous moon in
the thicket of an
almost bare tree.
Halloween.

*

Day moon over
the Art Institute.

How did it get
so big?

*

Moon—removing
her gray veil.

*

Not yet dark, the moon,
nearly full, with nimbus,
in a net of bare branches.

*

Gibbous moon
in black branches,
burning through
swiftly moving mist.

*

Hopping out of a
cab at Hollywood
and Clark: gibbous
moon in a cloudless
sky.

*

First Christmas
lights. No moon

for the longest time.

*

Crescent moon.
Then: a low plane.

*

Half moon, hazy,
directly over
the clock tower
at Dearborn Station.

*

Half moon, white
as a tooth, through
a mass of bare
swaying branches.
Shroud-like clouds
moving across.

*

Clear, icy
night. Gibbous
moon—white
and gleaming.

*

Byron sniffing

shoveled snow.
The moon, not
quite full, free
of branches by
the end of the block.

*

Same moon,
high in the sky,
lighting the ice-
tipped branches.

*

The moon—as full
as it can be and not
be full. Do the craters
make any shapes?

*

Full, horror film
moon, complete
with clinging branches,
shredded clouds.

*

A small faint dot,
barely burning through.

*

Waning, bright
and white.
Wintery.

*

Morning moon
in a slate blue sky.
Some of it was
eaten away
in the night.

*

Moon over
Manhattan.
It too is
far from home.

*

Quarter after midnight,
with Jeffery and Soraya,
corner of 9th St. and 6th Ave.,
the moon, its top
sheared off, above the building
where Balducci's used to be.

*

2:30 a.m., in Marcie's
kitchen window:
a crescent Cheshire

cat grin, rising
fast, above Denver's
twinkling lights.

*

I thought it was
the moon, but it
was a clock at the top
of a cell phone
tower.

*

The day after
Christmas. Home
from O'Hare.
Hello Byron!
Hello (half) moon!

*

Through the overcast:
a wedge of light
glowing, then dimming,
almost disappearing, then
glowing again.

*

A waxing, afternoon
moon.

8/1 – 12/28/06

Coyotes of Lakeshore Drive   KRISTY BOWEN

It was the worst sort of enchantment—
spring, and all the cherry trees on fire
in the park across the street. I had a bruised arm,
a polka-dot dress, and you, a canoe
in your garage we couldn't carry.
The morning was disguised
as a toothache and there was no getting over it.
We were the worst sort of accomplices,
replacing the arbor with tin cans
and tissue paper. The picket fence with chicken wire
until the evening spindled to an argument.
That night, I pulled enough hair from the shower drain
to make a doll, rode the bus home imagining feral shadows
moving in grass along the shoulder. Really, I was out for blood.
Biting your lip and moving over you in the orange glow of the streetlight,
something soft and fur-lined in my mouth when I kissed you.
We imagined horrible things were happening in the suburbs full of
key parties and discontented husbands.
Broken fences and children crouched in closets.
The boats in the harbor knocking sides in twilight.
The prairie stretching around us black and flat.

Birds of Paradise

RACHEL CONTRENI FLYNN

On the 96th floor
of the Hancock,
        you're amazed at the view,

but you must be subdued, as flawless
as flatware in your
        angular haircut, as bright as the glare

of chandelier against wineglass against Plexiglass.
An Allstate exec
        in monogrammed cuffs

says *This high up, the windows flex—*
they're synthetic. But he has such
        big teeth, you can't believe

you're safe and picture splinters of all that glass
blasting in when wind
        comes off the lake like a hatchet.

In the carousel of the city, birds of paradise
thrust up from centerpieces
        like switchblades

while single-file, the successful line up
for hand-carved slices
        of shoulder and butt, bleeding

under the warming bulb. They wag
their fingers, saying

Others are hungry

so keep moving up. Then they pass you
a toothpick
> in a crystal cup.

Ever since

HELEN DEGEN COHEN

the park is a dream
where we get down
into a paddle boat, all sweaty
from the whole trek from
across the oceans—Poland, Hungary,
Sweden, Everywhere Else
we were born in—and the heat
even on the cool grass around what
Americans call—pop.
                        We get down
into the funny little boat
and it goes, out, among the gardens and the little
green hills, and
        we run with movie magazines
        to the pool on the south side
        of the park, which is so big
        it has neighborhoods
        but it's Glenn Ford I like, not Ronnie
        Reagan, and we're all in love with
        Elizabeth T.
and this is the real thing, I'm walking
(ever since)
catty-corner across the park from Division
to (I'm reading The Wizard of Oz) the North Avenue
library, none such ever in what they call
"the old country", where I can get more than
10 books & do
(ever since, ever since)
catty-corner, back, between the gardens

and sit on the slope of a green hill
— this one's The Once and Future King
and there's no need to know English,
the words erupt "as they will" and string
themselves together somehow or other, and something
              like a story "comes to"—
on my sweater on the solitary spread of green
  catching more than a sunburn.
                        Sometimes
being alone is just like a long, slow kiss,
but it only happened in that one place
on that hill, overlooking the lagoon

we almost sledded into, in winter.
But that came later, it came second
or third, because first
              I'm walking, across the
only place in America I'm comfortable in,
the park, I'm "coming to," ever since,
heading for Kedzie where the green begins
and we girls sing.

Rising for the Buddha

DINA ELENBOGEN

Who falls onto the El with groceries for three
generations, who escaped pirates and prisons
to arrive in a place where a man sees
clotheslines of a different poverty
pass through a train window.
Who with wrinkles of sixty monsoons
lets a woman rise
from her seat for him
to replace her.
His fists are full with green onions
from the large gardens of a strange America
he takes home to a table
where everything and nothing
wait for him.

Chicago Harvest

MAUREEN TOLMAN FLANNERY

Fall, and the Waldorf School children
are weeding in the garden,
singing courage songs about St. Michael.
For Ramadan I went to a mosque
to help my Pakistani boss distribute
breakfast food to the few needy
and the many just waiting to eat.
A Mexican kid is building a sukkuh
for the lady on the corner.
She has me do it every year, he says.
It must be for something like Day of the Dead.
He winds grape vines around the poles
of his make-shift shed and thinks of his mother's grave,
bare or marigolds the years he's been here.
Tree sap recedes back to ground,
stalks go brittle and every green thing
trades its color for something closer to gold.
Air holds its leaf-smoky breath
and blows a little colder.

Missing Us   *MARY HAWLEY*

In terms of scale the sun is a pea next to the billiard ball
of Pollux, the flaming melon of Arcturus, and planet Earth
is invisible. Universally speaking we won't be missed.
But I am stuck in traffic on a city boulevard curving away

from a cold grey lake past train tracks, gas stations, schoolyards,
weedy lots dotted with half-finished condos while on the other side
of this world a giraffe stretches an impossible neck into the leafy bowl
of a tree. Since this is what we have we just might want to hold off

on ending it. Right now the air reeks with bitter notes of autumn
flowers and this city is not like Beijing or Lagos or Moscow; each
city has its own beating heart and chemical brain and mechanical
limbs. It is not like the ruins of Chan-chan outside Trujillo, Peru,

where long ago I languished all one afternoon as the wind blew me
a coat of dust and the dreary guide went on and on about the barren
plazas of sand that once rang, he said, with music and poetry. I
did not care about the eroded outlines of palaces or bone-dry

canals that irrigated the sunken gardens of the Chimu people
for five hundred years—what were they to me? Then. Five hundred
years ago this city was a swamp, and a dying giant in Perseus
burned with light that sparkles now over boulevards of fiery maples.

The Day is 7:03 AM, the Smoking Smart Car   MIKE PUICAN

a goldfinch. A girl walks her Chinese water dragon
             past the turquoise
        food processor left on the curb

by the stupid movers. She stops for the cadmium
             yellow school bus filled
        with dozing fifth graders. A flock

of larks banks left and almost
             disappears. Now notice
        the burnt sienna shoulder

of the woman crossing Logan Boulevard
             and her baguette.
        A mud-caked lawn mower falls

from a speeding pickup and rolls
             down the street.
        Someone go over and pull it to the curb!

Emptiness is primed with slate blues
             and maroons,
        fierce wills of dandelions

that brighten cracks in the sidewalks. The sun
             separates from the horizon
        just as the owner abandons

her burning Smart Car at the Quick-Mart, and spring
             makes beauty, throws it away,
        makes more.

Small Boy   MARC SMITH

Imagine a small boy doodling keys of a spinet piano in a red brick bungalow on the southeast side of Chicago

This was the rain ... *(he tinkles the high notes)* ... this was the thunder ... *(bang on the bass)* ... and this *(zing zing up and down the keyboard)* the electro-static stitches
knit now and again in the gray growing darkness gripping the sky.

    This was the bright blue ...
    ... the sun.
    Steps of a spider.
    Light on a downspout.
    Beads on the paint flakes
    Peeling off tin.

    This was the moon
    Dissolving in a window.
    Wrapping a shade,
    A passage of air.

    It moved the curtains,
    Sheer white from the wood sill
    Wet to the alley
    Caught in a spin.

    This was the cry
    Calling at midnight.
    Voiceless a cry
    Calling within.

These were the footsteps.
Someone was coming.
No one to listen.
No one to care.

He was a small boy
Running from father.
He was a father
Running to son.

They were a moment
Caught in a photo.
Caught in the sunlight.
Caught in a spin.

Here is the green lawn
Under the sunlight.
Green is the empire
Bounded by walks.

Here he is running
Fast through the red leaves
Falling in autumn
Into a pile.

Face of all sunlight
Passage through gangways
Taken at emergence,
Emergence to light.

This is the bright face,
Face of October,

Racing the summer
Indian ghosts.

Here are the brushed leaves
Frosted at morning.
Curling at sunset.
Curling in smoke.

This is the laced gown
Garment of snowfall
Flaking upon him
Falling within.

He was a small boy
Running from father.
He was a father
Running to son.

They were a moment
Caught in a photo.
Caught in the sunlight.
Caught in a spin.

This was the rain.
This was the thunder.
This was the lightning
Stitching the sky.

Here comes the dark blue
Backing the moonlight.
These are the stars spinning on high.
These are the stars spinning on high.

Storm Lessons   *PATRICIA MONAGHAN*

1. Somewhere, right now, one is brewing.

2. The wind is not trying to get in.

3. In high winds, songbirds sing.

4. It is not storms that rage and batter.

5. Butterflies migrate within.

6. The beauty of inky clouds
   over a churning white lake and
   the beauty of a still summer meadow
   are equivalent.

7. Storms storm. It's nothing personal.

8. They end.

July as a 1950's Sci-Fi movie   SUSEN JAMES

past curved glass the cicada's drowsy hum Lulu's skin
the sheen of beyond the window   when your breath lets go & you
become nearly invisible days
lost in the greenness

she looked to the moon as if it were her own face she
looked to the moon as if reading her obituary oxygen
no longer functioning the way it used to & they began to
appear like objects snared in the corner of eye

chrysanthemums exhaled to stunned
hands sure as any prophecy   overtime praying will leave
you thin as a nun   the air stiffened   Lulu listed on those south
thresholds like any orchard

unruly as a poet or something far less primitive
Go ahead alter my carbon she hollered in a good font for
            addressing
one's friends   lately everything has been happening to Lulu in the
3rd person   petals pelting

glazed from too little sleep Lulu's other worldly
sniffing   breaking crop circle codes to mathematics then
musical notation   chanted chains of vowels alert for nuances
swarming with bees

the moan of newly mown grass   the fish hook eyelid catch
of ivy   branches pricking at her face finger by curious
finger & flowers that bloom weapons
those roses   those thistles

Nocturnal

ALICE GEORGE

Animals could never
play us in this movie
because their eyes
are too elegant to believe

and they know no
trespass within this dark
zone, they own each
alley and mountain.

Here a woman grieves
for some indecipherable
grief worth a coloratura
so glottal we open

our purses desperate
for the right mint but find
all joy has been stolen.
Hearts blacken and whine

until we quit the opera
like a job that doesn't fit.
We look down at our bodies
and find that no matter

how we change our old skins
insist: freckled and so worn,
grey from the taxi's exhaust,
yet fragrant as if playing

and this is good, to search
down inside our clothes
and hold onto something
steady. Your hand swings

over in a boyfriend kind
of sway and we are mighty
walking down the street.
Wait, a gift, we are

the possums despite
what I said. We sing
long tones through the night,
rubbing sugar into our fur.

This Is to Find Out about Something   ARIELLE GREENBERG

Secret trip into the fat helium of O'Hare
        the chiming death-bell rainbow tunnel of Concourse C
        the tinging magic button blues of O'Hare

depart here and land here
        you would be home now
                if you were Chicago

                                      & you are Chicago
a bright keyed fog with a rose on the water tower

On the flat mountain-lack of Chicago
Miriam danced her girls around & tossed their silver bangles into pyre

who is the buckle on the belt of the bible Midwest
        Illinois word that collapses
                              state that falls down
flat into acreage of dark birds and Gods big & little too

This is to Find Out About Something

The you is over in an ocean or icecap, frenetic

Where is the moon and its mama   it is calling to its mama
        behind a building there

                        that's scraped the stars off

It is dirty but not dirty as some
It is noisy but maybe noisier than some (less honking)

It hath greater potential for owls

*

Wearing the Chicago coat, something freezy & friezed
in the moon of an Arctic bean, wedding cake'd bridge

forlon its lining   forlon blown   flapped
& bones as yet disintegrate

Butcher   Movie of the butcher and knife

Blow-hole to ship's prow   something happening   the Lake

Cite it down
             God-acre
             Forty acre
God it down silver moving skyscrape straightedge blade
         joust the sky of this deep coat

End now where thoust began: in a pocket
with the snowball gone to a holywater spot

         here's a cause (& effect): the babies
Go glue ribbons on the backs of your eyes for them
over Thanksgiving

        Be a peach in this frozen metal cage
Be a Michigan or a cherry with its stone still in
        the burst of grace congealed in a pin-drop
and that is how a baby is borned

Do not end with the wind or grey
        that is the name Chicago

Mechanical Foliage

JAMES SHEA

I felt the rapid turning of the sun in my direction.
I never saw this many squirrels at once.

A young entrepreneur sold me his business card.
He told me this was one of the beautiful days.

He offered a presentation on my whereabouts:
half of you awake, the other half was not asleep.

He said I would see handsome epiphanies,
a vision unifying the particulars, for example.

He put his hand up my sleeve and touched my chest.
In other words, it was a dream I still remember.

I heard sheets of ice clink over the lake.
I found the extraordinary moment and recorded it.

I wash small trees with my hands, sponging
the trunk and leaves. I live once supposedly.

Once the magnolia has blossomed   *ED ROBERSON*

   Once the magnolia blossoms,
the descending shadow of the petals
stains the street

   with the brown footprint leaving,
where it has stepped in itself,

   a track
walked in its own being flesh
gone as to excrement,

   Spring, in tomorrow's rain, comes,
a hose down of the annual
scene
       as of a murder,
the fallen petal

   of a sparrow
no one kept an eye on except
the peregrine
    from the Methodist church tower,

   a hose down and hope
this had to do with something
about the plant cycle

   of season done
               not sacrifice
to some lesser possession in blood
spent on the street,

   and so much lost   You'd think
beauty had left a lesson
     more   than there's more.

Brumation

KATHLEEN KIRK

After the dark flower
the woman

waited for the man
to shed his own burning skin.

Transplanted
she walked through woods in spring,

ribboned snakes writhing
beside bluebell, mayapple.

Years spiraled up
like smoke, black ash, from trash fires,

hardly noticeable after a breeze.
But the sifting had been done.

Harmless in the garden,
something

slithered away.

Blue Trees

LARRY JANOWSKI

They're spruces reigning roadside, three tall sisters
in a single net dress of needles, watered, fed blood

and crushed bone lithe and blue until men
in yellow hats insist *they gotta come down...*

the underground main. Piney scent scours
the street and the silence of a held breath spreads.

It can't be helped, my father's voice bounces room
to room. From the street he must seem to be singing.

The Fox

RICHARD JONES

Driving home from work,
the dark coming early
to the city in the rain,
shops and newsstands
neglected and derelict
under the streetlamps,
the muted metronome
of the wiper blades
ticking away the time,
I saw a fox dashing
along the embankment,
racing the lights
of the commuter train
chugging through the mist.
The intelligent eyes,
the slender face,
the lithe body,
the reddish tail
darted under
a chain-link fence,
disappearing
into a small wilderness
of rubbish and weeds
growing wild in the grim
shadows of the underpass—
a small piece of divinity
vanishing from sight
beneath the tracks
that carry the Skokie Swift.

Benched

E. ETHELBERT MILLER

It will be a day like this.
You will do all the things
you do in the morning
on the way to work. Just before
noon someone will inform you
that your job has been abolished.
You will clean your desk and office
and walk outside feeling numb,
angry and confused. You will
walk to a park and sit on a bench.
There you will imagine yourself
being homeless soon. You will
stare at the birds looking for food.

You will notice the birds for the first time.

In the Intersection, Jackson and State

TONY TRIGILIO

Without looking, I could cross Jackson
without getting struck, guided by voices, a hum
of tires on coarse pavement. I want to scale
one of those slopes, the blushed steel
of the CNA Building, grab the Monadnock's
frayed terra cotta drapery and climb.

Lakeside wind so loud it changes the subject.
In dreams, I lie too long on spring grass, pikes
still dead despite thaw. Ants crawl my arms,
bees swarm. Nature an antique, an abandoned
oak table behind glass, waiting for me
to test its legs, barter a price.

I'm afraid of nature. Orange, Brown Line
trains cross paths, the distant touch of negotiators.
Rivers changing course, office windows bound in mist.
Pavement accumulates, dismantles, rises; an array of noise
come again. One block east, a construction crew
is drilling, their hammers lift from State like smoke.

Wherever

VIRGINIA BELL

Cicada shrugs off its exoskeletal husk, lets it drop wherever
like a sweaty child whose jacket falls on the floor wherever.

Children refuse jackets because it's their mothers who are
cold; cicadas lose husks because they grow (or die) whenever.

I walked into your kitchen and saw that you had lined up a row
of large dead bees on the windowsill so they could live forever.

Still bees, luminous from light caught in stained glass wings,
their yellow black stripes become lines for writing whatever.

I watch your gloveless hands yank poison ivy from the yard,
remember how you went barefoot into city parks–I would never.

A woman walks out of an urban park with glass in her heel,
she bends over, pulls it out, keeps walking away to wherever.

Or there's the time you listened, cocktail in hand, to the man
who questioned the coherence of the rape victim's story, as if ever.

Then you spoke casually of a time so far back you remember it
as through a lid, that time a gun held you in a car going wherever.

You open old mason jars as I stand and listen in your kitchen,
fill the jars with virginia bluebells, and let the lids fall wherever.

One day

CECILIA PINTO

One day while walking the restless dog
I saw three graceful garter snakes
all dressed in black and orangey slip.
Two, wedded, slid beneath a wavering shrub.

The third, spinstered in a decaying stump
basked in her abandonment.

Night in a strange city

JULIE PARSON NESBITT

Chrysanthemums
yellow and white
like a Chinese funeral.

The scrawl of a cat's
voice against the sky.

Sticky, nocturnal
leaves release their scent.

The teeth of a scabby
dog scrape the moon.

Under the Full Crust Moon   MARTHA MODENA VERTREACE-DOODY

Sky cracks over the train yard edging I-55, clouds
the sycamore where the red-tail hawk
perches, trusting the storm to blow the pigeon
to his talons—another burst like a windshield showered
in a flail of gravel, slowing trucks
in the wrong lane, rush-hour traffic

                                  you try to avoid,
driving too fast. A coyote darts between stacked box cars
headed west or east—his grey coat
blending into dawn—

                        these days when sunlight thaws
what moonlight freezes—the swollen trail
      along Salt Creek where he would hunt—
and I turn up the news we listen to behind a red sea
                        of brakelights, the radio balks in static:
a half mile from Navy Pier an ice floe shudders
under nimble legs of a coyote whose desperate
hunger lures him to desperate places; smells the shoreline
he can find, belly full,
                     heavy lids of yellow eyes
tempting sleep, knows ice
can bear his weight alone, not firemen who trail him—

not the suck of air from a police helicopter
as it hovers over his island
                   when the break gives way—
he would have it this way—
divers held back by the snap underfoot,
shards of ice like melting arrowheads.

At first, fright;
                       then surrender to what comes next.

Ten minutes of climbing waves of slush
too deep to walk. Too cold to swim, he drifts,
beyond the pier, beyond the buoys,
                     sinks where no one can see to save him,

as the world fractures, I tell you.
We pick up speed.
You give the radio its final word
then turn it off.

Borders

ELISE PASCHEN

Behind our greystone on Oakdale

>a concrete landscape
>covers the ground.
>The alley shapes
>the letter *I*.

>Maneuvering
>into the aisle,
>I'm stuck. A neighbor
>flashes headlights.

>Parking is tight.
>We orchestrate
>our lives in such
>prized real estate.

>I execute
>a three-point turn
>into our drive.
>From air what patterns

>do we create
>down here? Against
>the back-deck's trellis
>violet clematis

>knots on the vine.
>Will it revive?
>Next-door a strip
>of earth which I've

witnessed transform,
despite exhaust
and lack of space,
from dirt to bloom,

continues each
spring to surprise,
illuminating
a manuscript:

the verdigris and rust outlining *I*.

Tree of Heaven

BARRY SILESKY

When I first came back to the city I wanted
to bring the chain saw. The scar
above my left knee, cut when a young oak fell
the wrong way in the woods I left was fresh.

I can still see the torn
jeans, the gap the chain
opened as it leapt by into the snow.
I stared at the wound, breath

gone smoke as blood spilled over the space.
but I was afraid I might use it, set the engine
roaring against garbage trucks, el trains
screeching past the porch, drunks

splattering bottles in the alley. I swore
this was no place to live. Then every June
catalpa's white flowers, October
berries of mountain ash, gaudy reds and golds

of all those immigrant plants painting
buildings, parks, lakeshore remind us
we do. And there's more. The latest storm blows
out over the lake. Leaves turn, fall, come back.

Years later I brought the saw here to trim
ailanthus and mulberry in my new front yard.
The engine needed work, the chain sharpening,
It woke the babies, the neighbors stared.

But I loved the country it brought me, power
filling hands, arms, skin, blotting
airplanes, traffic, rock 'n roll
screaming from the apartment across the street.

Now let that scum who snuck in our yard
to steal my bike show his face, the one who clipped
our tulips in their finest bloom a night last May.
The one who beat the old woman down the block.

They grow like weeds, these "trees of heaven"
that stink and spread everywhere,
their shade patches that won't cool
in some paradise no one believes. Roots thicken

under us, invisible ring by ring
until concrete and asphalt swell, buckle;
streets, walks, foundation walls lean and
break open. We've got to cut those trees

before they do their damage. The one on the edge
of the walk scraped our window,
split the short wall that holds back the neighbor's yard.
I want room for a flowering crab, its obscene flush

painting a week so delicious I can almost
taste flesh, flower, spring; or cherry, magnolia,
no matter what diseases those foreigners
might bring. Such May days feel

half the reason we live, and this year I'm going to
clear the junk, lose those extra pounds,

get to work. But I gave the saw away.
No time to keep the engine tuned, chain sharp

For the one day a year it might be used.
I took a bow saw up the ladder, balanced
in the first crotch, roped the bough to pull it
and cut the notch in front so it would fall

in our yard when I made the back cut.
Almost through, I stepped on the ladder, leaned
and held the other branch, sawed down.
And it worked: the familiar sweat and crack

as the bough broke off. Now the window's quiet
in the wind, but more than half that tree is
left, leaning over the deck next door.
The lower trunk's flush against the fence.

If I had the chain saw, I could cut a notch
work the tip into the back. I'd have to be
careful, fell it against its lean.
But the machine's long gone.

With only the bow saw, a ladder too short,
a little rope, I can't figure how
I'll get the rest of it down.
Last week someone sprayed a gang sign

on my back door. It looks like a fetus, blown up and
twisted beyond anything we can name.
This is my neighborhood, and I'm going to paint it
over, though I know they could be back any night.

They're everywhere. It looks like some version
of my initial. That scar on my knee's almost
gone now, but a dozen new twigs have broken
from the old trunk. No saw can stop it.

It Takes Particular Clicks

CHRISTIAN WIMAN

Flip-flops, leash-clinks,
spit on the concrete
like a light slap:
our dawn goon
ambles past, flexing
his pit bull. And soft,
and soon, a low burn
lights the flight path
from O'Hare,
slowly the sky
a roaring flue
to heaven
slowly shut.
Here's a curse
for a car door
stuck for the umpteenth
time, here a rake
for next door's nut
to claw and claw
at nothing. My nature
is to make
of the speedbump
scraping the speeder's
undercarriage,
and the *om*
of traffic, and somewhere
the helicopter
hovering over
snarls — a kind
of clockwork

from which all things
seek release,
but it takes
particular clicks
to pique my poodle's
interest, naming
with her nose's
particular quiver
the unseeable
unsayable
squirrel. Good girl.

Subdivision Ghazal

JAN BOTTIGLIERI

This is my street-song of praise for the neighborhood creatures.
In shadowways between houses creep neighborhood creatures.

The squirrel that plays at nonchalance; still rabbit, blurred bee.
Windowside, grey tree rustles with (it's understood) creatures.

The skunk that sprays; translucent aphid; rat-tailed possum
with shovel-smacked face. Our there-goes-the-neighborhood creatures.

Once a moon-glazed buck stepped from behind the Riveras' garage,
strode up the road, antlers raised like a torch for God's creatures.

Goldfinches, blue jays, red-tail hawks careening in like cops,
talons flashing: bright skyness of our neighborhood creatures.

Porchlights ablaze: what fiery night-eyes? What wide river
roaring? What does Wood Street display to the woods' creatures?

The lot lines, the mower ballets, the utility flags
flapping in rows (do they pray?)—yet in spite of grids, creatures.

In spite of grids, the malaise of chain-link, ornamental borders,
this poem: small, wild feet of the neighborhood creatures.

Unruly Urban Youth

BRENDA CÁRDENAS

When we slept in the back
bedroom of the ash-gray upper—
that little raincloud tucked
in a city park between cattails
at the duck pond's northern curve
and the locked down, fenced in
tenement we called a high school—
I woke each morning at 6 a.m.
to the squawks and screaks
of baby robins hanging
by Christmas tinsel and twigs,
helicopter seeds and shredded
test scores, leaves, love notes
patch-worked and tree-sapped
to the metal awning that pinged
when pecked, screeched like a chalk-
board against claws. Such ruckus,
such shrill panic in hunger's
unruly demands for nurture
or escape, such riotous music
thundering my eyes open
just in time to watch two tiny deer
appear in the bushes of your hair,
both decked out in their full regalia—
their clattering racks of antlers.

What Garfield Park Kept Saying

PATRICIA SMITH

No one skated. No one could skate. In fact,
we had very specific ideas concerning blades,
and our feet were never involved. My mother
absently sucked the loose gold that framed
her left front tooth while slicing into the thickness
of some pig for the necessity of supper. Daddy
carried a quick-flick razor in the side pocket
of pencil-legged pants, just waitin' for some
fool to get wide on whiskey, slyly palm the ace
and get cut. In my room off of other rooms,
I danced slow around the edges of paper dolls,
scared to slip and slice recklessly into blonde flips
or perfect pink legs. The idea of chilly dance,
the snowy felt skirt with its flouncy curled hem,
of lacing up in stiff white leather and scissoring
gracefully on dirty ice past storefront preaching
and gin mills, of lifting up one leg and spinning
like a hot whisper and not even falling, the idea
was hurtful because one more time I had to reach
so far outside my own head to even think that way.

But from the layered gray greenness of the park,
a recorded monotone kicked in, 10 pm every night,
plodding until dawn. *Danger. Do not go on the ice.
Danger. Do not go on the ice.* Oh, that's left over,
daddy said, from the days when young Jews twirled
gleefully into and out of the arms of one another,
passing time while their fathers coaxed thick music
from bulky phonographs and their mothers fiddled
with the perfection of place settings. At night, the ice,

suddenly more water than anything, impenetrable
beneath the moonwash, would call again to them.
Occasionally a skater would crack the lying surface,
flail beautifully, scream into the pocket of dark,
and drown. The deep bellow was designed to repel,
to gently enter their blood, to convince them of sleep.

So during the day, I'd scurry past the line of swings
singing out their rust, the boys who leaned toward
my running to whisper a symphony of the word *pussy*,
the frightened manless mothers arced like rooftops
over their ashy screeching children, and I'd look
hard for the rink, a golden gleam beneath the napped
weeds and slush. One time I thought I sensed a faint
outline, a soft bean-shaped impression, muted and
glamorous, but there was nothing to be resurrected,
no water to freeze and glisten and beckon. The nightly
admonition, measured and chill, kept riding uselessly
on the air, disturbing Negroes in their sleep. But deep
in the center of winter, ragged little circles of flowing
would freeze and shine, and I became obsessed, finding
and standing on them, pushing with the full of my weight,
jumping even, playing my ace, trying to win some game
by being white, beautiful, tragic and dead all at once.

Entering Strange Cities   ALLAN JOHNSTON

"The erection itself is not incompatible with the system"
*   —Jean Baudrillard*

        Entering the strange cities,
one finds the trees that are reaching up like supplicating hands,
or only like the branches that grow toward the light from beyond the
  world.

        Or else there are no trees;
the lights of the city drone over empty streets like homeless bees.
Emaciated figurines reach up to catch the baseballs of light. Or else
there is no light. The buildings are dark, their strata founder
in rows of windows, or the sides of the factories pound, or in suburbs
cities are named and hum
as images on television sets, cities are dreamed of as if they too
were real, for
to use the tongue
to scent a path
through ideas
requires signs,
and these, significant
or other, call forth
the glottals,
rituals of slobber,
the waves the eye sees as water
edging up or moving through the city in incandescence.

This is the central monument: the carved statue of the hero;
under it, the child, a part of no statue, addicted, falling
apart. In other places the mutant man is moving —

> look onto the streets of any city where trees lift like hands,
> or only as trees;

look where the loosened suitcase flops on the sidewalk in the small
disasters of the tourist; look where someone wears eyeglasses
as thick as porcelain, wide eyed; in the swimming shift of light
each hand is reaching toward a different end. The chameleon
line of the blinded eye strikes as he reads the braille book,
one hand moving across the page in English, one in Arabic,
and the book ripples, its thick pages wattled like turkey skin,
three fingers flying one way, one the other, and the sense of it all
in the touches nonchalantly bent, a birdlike flight of the hand
entering the strange city in an unfamiliar way,

by vehicle or path, for each road separates how one is approached
in cities as much as how one approaches. One finds the trees that are
> rising
like supplicating hands,

or else one only finds the trees that still are lifting branches
toward the light from beyond the world. Or else one finds

> > no trees,
> > for some cities
> > work to topple trees,

to bring the freedom no tree brings,
the high, cracked love of buildings;

the factory of winds that move fiercely
across the frozen lands.

Hawk Hour

MARK TURCOTTE

In this city time unwinds in unnatural ways. It doesn't even fly. It trips. It passes in coughing fits. It doesn't have enough soul to tick tock tick. It spits and spews under the rusty fenders of all these cars going nowhere fast. It's bad for the body. Even here at the corner of Sheridan and Pratt, the lake and its waves only a block away, I cannot measure my dying. Instead, this taxi pants at the traffic light. Instead, this bus, the Outer Drive Express, lodges in my ventricle. This city breaks my clock.

On my good leg I wobble between the I-pods wearing all those heads wearing the same 2.8 million faces. Some idiot calls it a river of humanity but rivers don't move like this. It's not natural. I stagger past the café that wasn't here yesterday, won't be here tomorrow. Past the liquor store that will be here forever lubricating the gears and all their broken teeth. I lurch past the rows of trees. Gnarled sticks attacked by choking leaves. Near the Red Line tracks a squad car screams *up against the wall* to people already up against the wall. I give away a dollar to a man who says *god bless*.

In Loyola Station I hand two-twenty-five to the turnstile. It says nothing. I crawl up the escalator at 90 miles per hour, blur to the end of the platform at 95. I pause in a still shadow that has draped itself across my eyes. I catch my breath, stand upright. Above me the shape of a hawk drowns out the sound of the next ten trains and with its beating wings reaches out to stop the sky.

Windy City

CHRISTINA PUGH

They wrote all over the rocks, the ones
who came before and come still; choicer
than graffiti, the paint cubed and letters
blocked like epitaphs: *Acid* or *small groove*
or *baby cakes.* And primary colors whet
the schools of foam the lake makes,
its mobile cursive less serene, while the city
wells above that trace of sociability—
its steeples snuffed, or nearly, in the mist:
this could have been Christminster,
or these the moral rocks Tess read
on her journey home in terrible,
delicate boots: the shores mirror us
always, but the city transpires.

Look at you. *DOLORES WILBER*

Born and raised in Chicago, I live in the heart of the city. I constantly know and don't know the city I've lived in for fifty years. Like most people who live in an intensely urban culture, the city I grew up in is a distant, achy memory, and I know that I am not from this place any longer, as much as I love what I love. I am fortunate to be able to travel often to different parts of the world, to experience different urban environments. This work derives from my interest in issues of personal space, interpersonal relationships and the home, particularly home as a site of knowledge as well as personal comfort and sustenance. Knowledge of my physical and emotional space in isolation does not provide enough information, a flatland lacking the intersection of my friends from other places. I invited several collaborators from Portugal, Amsterdam, China, England, Israel and Estonia to participate, providing a deep mapping of a personal space of their choice by video, sound, text or image. My contribution to this collaboration resulted in a video and photographic essay; the latter featured here, entitled "Look at you."

Look at you.

DOLORES WILBER

Just look at you
an experience
a true bit
a breath
with someone
dear to me.

Pulling out of waiting
laying on the grass
tracing the clover
rooting it out
in favor of the proper lawn
impossible
do-able
and maybe we will find
the lucky four-leaf clover.
The shrill whistle
signaling
get home right now
you
mine.

Not mattering so much.

Little trees conquered
and big trees foreboding and not conquered
drifting in space
apparitions lit up by the encounter.

That's it.

URBAN NATURE POETRY, PROSE & PHOTOGRAPHY 105

"41° N, 87° W,(Chicago)" *MARY JANE DUFFY*

size: 50 x 50",
materials:acrylic on canvas
date completed: 2010

My most recent series of paintings and drawings are abstracted landscapes that investigate the relationship between humans, nature and technology. We continue to destroy the natural world, creating an environment that is ever more artificial. New technologies allow us to live our lives at an increasingly frenzied pace. Photographic satellite images taken from Google Earth are transformed into painted flat shapes with a limited color palette.

Flat shapes are a reference to the digital, mathematical vector shapes as opposed to continuous tone of a photograph, or the way we see. I became particularly interested in flatness while reading Tom Friedman's *The World is Flat*. The author describes globalization as making places placeless-multinational, virtual. In addition to flatness, shapes ooze and creep, creating an eerie quality.

Colors in these paintings range from bright to very dull. Natural colors like blues and greens are a reference to the natural environment, while murky, dull colors are a reference to how we have transformed our environment. Bright, unnatural colors are a reference to human-made environments, like bright colors of city, but also personal experience. The bright lines are the paths I have taken through a place. Places chosen as source material are sites to examine the tension between the personal, national, global and natural. This painting is based on a Google Earth satellite photo of Chicago. I have lived here almost my entire life.

September 2010

URBAN NATURE POETRY, PROSE & PHOTOGRAPHY

Predation

LIAM HENEGHAN

ID_BAN NATURE POETRY, PROSE & PHOTOGRAPHY   109

Eden Extracts *MARK CURRAN*

'You ask me about a future and seeing a future…I have problems seeing it or sensing it.'
(Konrad, student, Cottbus, September 2007, original in German)

BRUTE NEIGHBORS

URBAN NATURE POETRY, PROSE & PHOTOGRAPHY 111

Elston Avenue, Rogers Park, Montrose Harbor

RANDALL HONOLD

URBAN NATURE POETRY, PROSE & PHOTOGRAPHY 113

BRUTE NEIGHBORS

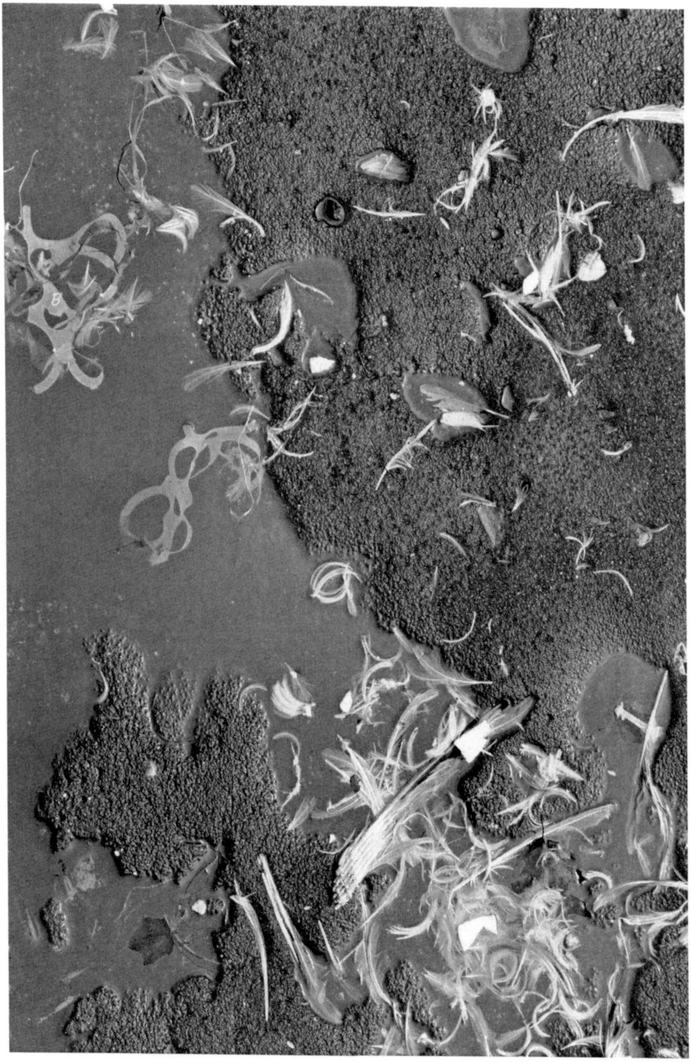

17-Year Itch   *MILES HARVEY*

"Look, Daddy, look here," my nine-year-old yelled, and when I turned she was crouching on the sidewalk, pointing to a pair of insects, their abdomens interlocked, their tiny flame-colored eyes aglow with what I could only presume was pleasure. "Daddy look, they're fighting," she exclaimed, and I said they weren't fighting, and she asked what they *were* doing, and I said they weren't fighting. Here it comes, I thought, that discussion I had been hoping my wife would get to handle. But no, the girl let the matter drop, perhaps because she was having so much fun flicking her forefinger at the two-headed monster, or perhaps because she found it impossible to converse amid the roar coming at us from us at all directions, a roar that I would later learn measured upwards of 90 decibels, as loud as a bus or a bulldozer, only it didn't sound like a bus or a bulldozer, but the waste disposal of a kitchen sink, if, that is, you happened to leave a spoon in the drain and then you happened to amplify the whole thing through a massive stack of arena-rock speakers.

This was June of 2007, and I had returned to Downers Grove, the western suburb of Chicago where I grew up and my elderly mother still lives, so that my two young children might experience the miracle of the 17-year cicadas. Yes, miracle—an object of wonder, a marvel, an event beyond rational comprehension. For what could be more miraculous than to find the familiar streets of your quiet hometown utterly transformed, the sky black, the groomed lawns convulsing, the trees swarming with 17-year cicadas in heat, or whatever it is 17-year cicadas are in when they emerge from their long adolescence beneath the soil, shed their skin, pair off, plant eggs and die? I read somewhere the population density for that particular brood has been estimated as high as 1.5 million per acre—meaning, if my own rough calculations are correct, that we squashed upwards of 27 insects with every new step. There was no stretch of sidewalk or soil not pulsing with insects *in flagrante delicto*, no branch, no leaf, not littered with abandoned bug husks. The spectacle was as overwhelming to our eyes as the howl was to our ears. And then, just when it seemed as if they were absolutely everywhere, we came upon a place where they were even more everywhere than everywhere else.

This tree—encrusted with exoskeletons that shimmered like the jeweled walls of the Taj Mahal—stood right around the corner from the house where my mother grew up in the 1930s, and just down the street from the one in which I spent my youth, the yellow Victorian my family has owned since 1964. It was not one of the iconic trees of my childhood, like the huge willow that hung over Prince Pond, its fronds slapping our faces as we skated through them on frigid afternoons, or the craggy oak under which my brother and I played our first games of wiffleball, or the invincible elm that survived both a killer blight and a lightning strike, the scar from which still runs down its trunk in my mother's backyard. To be honest, I cannot recall whether the tree I am now attempting to describe was a locust or a maple, a chestnut or an ash. Although I walked beneath its tall branches thousands of times, I took notice of it exactly once—the moment when my daughter and my son and I stopped and stood in awe before its great, swarming trunk, the bark of which appeared entirely made of bugs. For horny cicadas, this was sin city, the place where you could check your inhibitions at the door and unleash a decade and a half of pent-up desire. Like the famous slogan goes, what happened at that tree stayed at that tree—though eventually, as my children and I observed, it wound up in a crunchy pile of corpses at the base of that tree. And yet despite the stench of bug rot, which hung sweet and metallic in the air, I knew even then that I was witnessing something sublime—sacred shrine and sex club, Vegas and Vatican rolled into one, the great tree of cicada life, touching the heavens that summoned those insects every 17 years and reaching deep into the earth from whence their curious journey began.

Later, when we left the blare of the bugs for the quiet of my mother's house, I felt a surge of nostalgia as we came through the door. The slate floor of the front hall, made from classroom blackboards my late father had salvaged from an elementary school where he taught; the smiling portraits of my parents some artist had sketched a half-century earlier; the chipped plaster bust of a little girl reading, the photograph of a younger, thicker-haired version of myself, wearing an Elvis Costello T-shirt and petting a dog who has been dead for at least 25 years—these everyday objects, most of which I had not stopped to contemplate for decades, now seemed strangely comforting and potent, as if they had power to slow down time, guard the house against the storm of life and sex and death thundering outside. And I felt grateful that my children had not been born too late to know this decrepit old house, grateful that its musty odor, distinct from the musty odor of every other decrepit old house in the world, would linger forever in that part of their brains where smell meets memory, just as it would in mine, and grateful, above all, that they loved these trips from the city to visit my mother, that despite a difference in age of 75 years, they considered her a close friend and confidante.

She listened intently to their stories of the cicadas, but declared that she had no interest in being out among those horrid little beasts. It still made her wince to remember how the great-great-great grandparents of this current batch of bugs had invaded the town in 1939, when she was a girl of 15. She didn't like the sound of them and she didn't like the look of them and she didn't like the feel of them. If one of the insects happened to land on her, it made her skin crawl. Better to be inside, she insisted.

But she and I both knew it was not the cicadas that kept her in the house that afternoon. Now 86 years old, slowed by arthritis, emphysema, heart disease, dementia and a growing list of other complaints, my mother is no longer able to stroll the streets on which she grew up, wander the neighborhood where she has spent all but a few years. Even climbing stairs has become a daunting task, so she spends her nights on a bed in the dining room and most of her days behind the thick doors of that old house, a 24-hour news channel shaking the walls at full volume because she is so hard of hearing. No doubt she would be safer, more comfortable and perhaps even happier at a retirement home, but she insists on staying put. Like the bugs she so despises, she was born of that soil, has spent her brief moment on earth there, and has no urge to die anywhere else.

The ancient Chinese, I have read, had a custom of placing a small jade amulet, fashioned in the form of a cicada, on the tongue of a dead person. The idea was to help the immortal soul break free of the body, just as the cicada sheds its skin and flies away after emerging from the soil. Even today, people in China still associate cicadas with regeneration.

It's an apt symbol, I suppose, and yet there's something that troubles me about it, this idea that eternal bliss only comes from casting off one's old shell. In my mother's front hallway is a placard that reads *These Are the Good Old Days*. She is not the sort of person who tacks sentimental aphorisms on her walls, but this one has been there for decades and means a lot to her. A lifelong Democratic Party activist and veteran of endless liberal causes, she has done her best, even after my father died in 1986, not to wallow in the past or dream of better times ahead but to make herself useful in the here and now. Still, on a recent visit home, I couldn't resist asking if she contemplates what comes next.

"What good does it do to think about it?" she replied with a laugh. "What point is there in getting excited about whether there's an afterlife or not? Maybe yes, maybe no."

She has never been particularly interested in matters of faith, attending a Unitarian church more for a sense of community than to fill any deep spiritual need. Nonetheless, she said, she can't help hoping that the end is not really the end, that her story still has more chapters. "I've been very fortunate, and I have lived a long, long time, and I know that—and I'm willing to live a long, long time from now on, too."

As for what her idea of eternity might entail, she could offer no concrete image. "I haven't got a very great imagination," she protested. "I mean, everybody who is religious seems so damn sure of everything." But when I pressed her on it, she spoke of a desire to remain with her family and friends, to watch her grandchildren grow up. As we sat there sipping coffee from chipped cups that have been on her shelves for as long as I can recall, it occurred to me that her idea of the sweet hereafter looked exactly like this house.

The next time the cicadas return, my children will be adults, perhaps with children of their own, and I will be 63, older by two years than my father when he died of cancer. The house on Linscott Avenue will have been standing for 133 years, if it makes it that long, which seems unlikely. My wife and I can't imagine living in the suburbs, nor can my brother, and real-estate agents inform us that any buyer would be likely to tear the place down, partly because it needs so much work and partly because it sits between two lots, on which a developer could double his profits by building a pair of new homes. And sometimes I think that would be for the best. In middle life I have begun to make peace with the idea that nothing lasts, not even that tree at the end of my mother's street. I was visiting her one afternoon not long ago when I noticed it was gone. There wasn't even so much as a stump, just a mound of woodchips, oblong and solitary, like a freshly covered grave. I am no tree-hugger, much less insect-lover, no stranger to chainsaws or cans of Raid. Perhaps that tree had to be taken down. Perhaps its time had simply come. And yet there are certain nights when, awaiting sleep's slow arrival, I find myself haunted by the thought of those bugs rising through the soil and emerging into the light, their instincts suddenly failing them, the object of their lifelong quest nowhere to be seen, like a man who awakens in the middle of his journey to discover he no longer knows the way home.

Boy Eats World   MICHELE MORANO

In the spring, it takes a long time to walk down the street, past the budding maple trees and bare, scaly-barked sycamores that line our side of the block. By early summer, leaves will scrape against our apartment windows, their branches entwining above the middle of the street. But in spring the sun is barely filtered, the world painfully bright. The sidewalk crawls with ants and the occasional earthworm, marooned after last night's rain. A squirrel stands on hind legs, craning its neck toward us and chattering.

We're not getting anywhere. Not that we *have* to get anywhere, but the plan was to walk to the park. To swing and climb and drive the wooden fire engine. To run through the grass because I think children should run through grass every single day if they can. Still, I'm adaptable. I could spend the next hour on this block, examining the beetle heading up a wrought-iron fence, loading our pockets with wet stones. But the slower we move, the more dangerous the street becomes.

Andrew is almost two years old. Everything in this enormous world exists for him alone. He lumbers toward the brazen squirrel, arms outstretched. He pinches the beetle and carries it, tiny legs kicking, toward his lips. He waits until I glance away, at a large dog dragging its owner toward us, and pops a stone into his mouth. "No, honey, no," I say, trying to remember how to save a choking toddler. When the dog approaches, Andrew squirms away from me and greets him, tongue to tongue.

So I hurry him along. "Not in the mouth, crazy man" is my constant refrain. But so much captivates him! Around the corner on Glenwood Avenue, gardens line the narrow parkways between the sidewalk and the street. Here are clumps of prairie weeds, flowering hostas, tiny new impatiens. Andrew trudges, palm open, slapping the plants, and when a leaf or a flower sticks to his finger, he licks it off. "No!" I say. "Spit!" Because there are poisons, too, along a city street. Jimsonweed, rhododendrons, jack-in-the-pulpits, pokeweed – all potentially toxic to a two-year-old. Not to mention unsanitary, since these curbside gardens are where dogs pee.

Throughout the spring and into the summer we walk to the park, and every chance Andrew gets, he eats. If we run into a friend, if I start to chat and take my eyes off him for a few moments, I find bits of mulch around his mouth, hear him sucking on dandelion stems. Once, a small hunk of dessicated poop, so old it's almost white, brushes his moist lips before I swat it away.

Then, as June turns toward July, as we pare down to shorts and sunscreen and stick to the shade, berries appear. Everywhere. Some grow on bushes, miniature blueberries that the birds don't touch. Some look like round strawberries, or holly berries or plastic beads, and each time Andrew reaches for one, I repeat the mantra, "We don't eat those." Then one day Andrew bends over the sidewalk just outside the park and points. The concrete is purple with juice, and whole berries squash under our sneakers. I look up to the source, a mulberry tree in the front yard of a two-flat.

Suddenly I'm thinking of an afternoon years ago, in graduate school, when a couple of friends and I were walking over a bridge. This was in a small city, early in what I didn't know would become a long period of urban dwelling, without a yard of my own, without space to garden. Beside the bridge, on a sloping bank, stood a white mulberry tree, its branches hanging over the guardrail toward us. "Look at all these pale berries," one of my friends said, and I stopped dead. Years before, I'd lived in a house in upstate New York, on property filled with raspberries, blackberries, mulberries both red and white. I'd filled buckets with them, baked pies. I'd eaten mulberries on my cereal in the morning, delighted by how easy it was to walk down the driveway and pick from the lower branches, like shopping outdoors.

In the moment of recognizing the white mulberries, of seeing for the first time what I'd been hurrying past every day, I became attuned to the scent of warm, weedy foliage along the bank and the sun on my arms. Everything about the street and the afternoon shifted. The accordion of time collapsed, and a younger version of myself reached up, plucked a berry from the branch and popped it into my mouth. Food, growing right here on a city street! I laughed aloud, my friends horrified.

How long ago all of that seems now, on this Chicago afternoon, red mulberries splashed across the ground and my two-year-old holding one out, eyebrows arched in question. What I want to say is: Eat, my love, they're good for you. But two days ago his father came home with a confession. They'd been looking at a bush with pretty red berries when, quick as lightening, Andrew picked one, stuffed it into his mouth, and swallowed. "Little red berries," his father said. "Bright red. But he seems fine."

"OK," I said, deciding not to panic. "And he ate just one?"

His father looked toward our milk-faced, guilty boy. "One at first. But I didn't realize he'd put some in his pocket, and on the way home he ate those, too."

I threw my arms into the air and shouted, "Crazy man, you ate the berries?"

Andrew giggled and nodded with great energy. I made a show of scolding him and his father both, karate-chopping the air and slapping the sides of my head. Then I pulled Andrew onto my lap and explained that the berries might make him sick. He might get a bellyache and have to go "blech! blech!" into the toilet. And if that happened, we would go to the hospital. I did not search the Internet until weeks later, which was a good thing or we would have gone to the hospital right then.

I can't teach a two-year-old to eat mulberries but not yew berries, a mere three of which can interrupt his heart rate. Some day, maybe, but right now I have to tell him no, icky, put the berry down. And because he's maturing, he does. We squat side by side and study the sidewalk, and I describe the bowl of raspberries at home in the refrigerator, waiting for us. But I don't feel good about this. I'm teaching him to fear the natural world, to see it as inferior to the man-made one. Berries from the fridge are better than berries from a tree. What kind of nonsense is that?

One of my own earliest memories is of being just a little older than Andrew, three maybe, and defying my mother's instructions not to eat plants. We lived in an enormous house then, because early childhood homes are always enormous, with a grand backyard bordered by a stone retaining wall. Atop the wall were flowerbeds, and out of the cracks between the stone grew the most delicious, flowering stems. They had thick, needle-ish leaves and smelled dark, forbidden, like freshly dug earth. Whenever the little girl across the street came to visit, she and I ate the stems, even though my mother had caught us several times, had spanked me, and I'd promised never to touch them again. But the moment she went into the house – to answer the phone or tend to something on the stove – we ate. We picked little pieces, an inch long or so, then ran a few feet away and pretended to play. After a moment one of us would say, "Want some more?" and the other would nod with excitement. Decades later, I remember vividly the excitement of satisfying my own desire rather than my mother's wishes. I remember the texture – snappy, juicy – and the taste, which was sweet, then slightly bitter, then sweeter by contrast, propelling me again and again toward the wall. I ate the forbidden fruit as often as I could, and the lesson I learned then is one I carry along the street today, nothing happened.

And yet I've read and heard enough stories in which children gnaw on leaves or twigs and terrible things happen to them. So I stay vigilant, vowing to learn more about what grows along our daily paths and, in the meantime, repeating over and over again that distasteful word, "No."

Late one afternoon in the fall, Andrew's father and I pick him up from daycare and head to the park. It gets dark early now, but winter's coming and we all need to feel the grass under our feet for as long as we can. Except that lately the grass is covered with long, brown, leathery seed-pods. Andrew picks one up and aims it at us, singing, "pssh, pssh, pssh." Everything is a fire hose to this boy – his father's belt, my bathrobe tie, a kitchen towel stretched on the diagonal. No matter that the seed pod is only six inches long.

At daycare, the kids have been studying the growing season. They sprouted seeds, planted them, and are now learning about the harvest, so I kneel down and explain the way trees reproduce. I show Andrew how to tear open the paper-thin pod and find the seeds. "Like green beans," I say, "but these seeds make new trees. And we don't eat them."

Andrew doesn't even like green beans, although he enjoys aiming them at the cat and squeezing. But now, as if a switch has been turned, he extracts seed after seed and tosses them into his mouth, scrambling away from me, running and trying to open the next as he goes, laughing and dodging. "No!" I shout, "Yuck!" but I'm laughing, too, remembering my own early feast. Sometimes the hardest part of parenting is resisting seduction. Because who doesn't want to abandon reason and eat the world? Who doesn't want to take it all in, literally? Especially here in the city, where the rules are many and varied – stop signs, walk lights, public and private space. I chase Andrew, pull the pods from his hands, say, "Spit, crazy man, spit!" but what I really mean is: Don't be afraid. Resist adult worries, ignore the worse-case scenarios, and eat.

Later I learn that the seed pods are from honey locust trees, not only perfectly edible but a staple of Native American diets. And the forbidden fruit that's remained in my tongue's memory all these years? Portulaca. The uncultivated kind, which is less sweet and succulent than its refined cousin, purslane, but still perfectly good in salads or stir-fries. It, too, grows in our neighborhood, creeping along the border of a raised flower bed in someone's front yard. There for the tasting.

Plain Scared, or: There Is No Such Thing as Negative Space, the Art Teacher Said S. L. WISENBERG

In a college art class I learned that negative space was the nothing behind the figure you were looking at. But years later another teacher told me that this was not so. There is always something there, he said. If you look, you will see it.

Kenophobia is the fear of empty rooms. Fear of empty places. Agoraphobia is the fear of open places. But it *is* not the agora, the marketplace, that frightens me. I am not afraid to leave the house. I am afraid to leave the city. To be more precise—to venture from the SMSA (Standard Metropolitan Statistical Area).

I live on the North Side of Chicago. I find the word "kenophobia" in a book in the main library of Evanston. About twenty years ago, I lived in a dorm room in Evanston. The room was empty when I arrived and empty when I left. I remember one June I kept a university library book almost until the minute the taxi came to take me to the airport. I wanted to keep, as long as possible, some connection with the place I was leaving empty.

I am afraid of being erased. One night in a lover's apartment, after he told me he didn't want to see me any more, I left this note in his desk: I was here. I was once a part of your life. He has since moved to a condo. I do not know what became of the desk.

We are all afraid of being erased. Our names in water writ. Of the earth disappearing. We are small and the night looms.

The night ends. The prairie goes on forever. A sameness, for the uninitiated, the way all the seasons in Miami seem alike to newcomers. I am uninitiated.

We all fear the blank page, the blank mind dry of thought.

In and around Chicago, experts are replanting *the* prairie. I think this involves both public and private funds. I like reading about such things. I don't mind walking through these prairies if they are small and surrounded by city. It's the big areas I don't like; I don't like to hike. I like to walk through cities, looking in store windows.

I grew up in Texas, came to the Midwest at 18. I grew up with ranch houses and sidewalks. I loved taking the bus downtown and walking among abandoned railroad cars, buying old records in a shabby pawnshop. I'd eat lunch at Woolworth's and buy make-up at Neiman-Marcus.

In my 20s I moved from Illinois to Iowa to Florida back to Illinois. In Iowa I liked the pale green bowls of hills along the highway. I admired them from behind the windows of cars. The hills looked like paintings. In Miami in the newspaper office where I worked, we worshipped the sun from afar. During particularly dramatic sunsets, we reporters would stand near our desks, looking through the windows closest to us, facing west, waiting, watching.

My only forays into nature are very tame—residencies at artists' colonies. I have to pack along piles of little white tablets made of cortisone. When my asthma's bad I take the pills for eight or nine days in a row. I'm allergic to nature. Ragweed, grasses, mold, spores, hay, milkweed—things I can name and things I can't name.

The first artists' colony I went to had once been Edna St. Vincent Millay's retreat a few hours from Manhattan—strawberry farm, hills, pond, trees. At Millay, I learned what foxglove was, and phlox, learned how to spot jack-in-the-pulpit and lady-slipper, all veins and sex. The colony's assistant director told me about a New York artist who had come to the colony and had walked around the grounds a while. Then he'd fled inside and reported that he'd seen an animal. What was *it!* she'd asked. He didn't know. He couldn't tell whether it was a squirrel or a deer.

During my residency, there were two painters who gushed over the landscape. They tried to match the colors of nature with the colors of paint. Cerulean Blue? they would ask each other, pointing at the sky. Havannah Lake?

It is land. It is only land.

The assistant told me that the pioneers from the East feared the flat open land of the West. For some of them, the horizon was too large. They couldn't see themselves in it. They were diminished. Some Easterners returned. Some carved themselves into the Western landscape.

***

I am not from the East but I understand those Easterners. I don't like limitless horizons. I don't embrace endless fields. I like nature with borders.

The plains scare me.

I am plain scared.

I am terrified of the universe that has no end. I am afraid to step behind the curtain, ask, What is the system behind this solar system? And behind that.

There is no negative space, only positive space having a bad day.

Franz Kafka was born in a city and was buried there. In 1912 he wrote: Ever since childhood, there have been times when I was almost unhappy about my inability to appreciate flowers. This seems to be related in some way to my inability to appreciate music.

I like flowers. A flowerbed is not the same as a field. Which life depends on. Wildlands are beautiful, they say. They must be saved. There is music in the prairie, they say.

Kafka is less foreign to me than Wendell Berry. I feel closer to Mikhail Zoshchenko's Moscow of the bureaucratic 1920s, than Larry McMurtry's Texas.

I find myself inside books by writers who write in fast, urgent sentences with no time for landscape. Writers of closeup conversations—internal and external—writers of the life of streets, cafes, stores, restaurants. Writers who rent. But there are others, so many others; I am not always curled up with my own kind. But I skip the parts, all the parts, about nature.

When I was younger, my friends and I would find books with sex in them. We would read those parts aloud, skip everything else.

Therefore, nature is the opposite of sex.

I know two women in Western Michigan who like to read farm novels. One of them has tiny plastic cows and horses super-glued to her dashboard. I don't think I've ever read a farm novel, though I imagine myself finding pleasure in following the slow quiet rhythms of crops pushing their way skyward, in descriptions of the dirt and sweat and dampness of stables, the lowing and groaning. Pure, sweet tiredness after you latch the door, blow out the lantern.

***

I was at the late Kroch's and Brentano's bookstore on South Wabash Avenue. A street with the same name as a river, believed to be taken from the Miami Indian word for "gleaming white." At the bookstore I picked up a book, *A River Runs Through It*. A sleeper of a book reissued, glamorized by Hollywood. It is my friend A.'s favorite book. I never talk to A. anymore because he met his ex-girlfriend through me. Somehow that is a problem though we were never lovers. These are the sorts of things I write about—things that happen indoors. I like A.'s writing, respect his judgment. But I didn't buy the book. I was afraid I would not enter it, afraid of some flatness of surface, nothing to hold onto. Like being afraid to enter into a conversation with a person who has a difficult accent or an unfathomable expression; scratch and scratch and still there may be nothing there.

(But so many other people liked the book. A. loved it, and he's from Manhattan. He likes to fish.)

Or like being afraid of sex, afraid to enter its raw territory, afraid I will find myself in the middle of it, not want to be there, and feel alone, terribly alone, too aware of my surroundings.

Many years ago I had an internship in Downstate Illinois at the *Quincy Herald-Whig*. I made friends with a young reporter there from a smaller town. She told me, All cities are alike. She didn't see the point in going to more than one of them.

I use free address labels from the Sierra Club and Nature Conservancy. I am not a member. Over the years I've joined the National Trust for Historic Preservation and the Chicago Architecture Foundation. I used to love the before and after spreads in magazines on restored opera houses, movie theaters saved from the wrecking ball and transformed into quaint shopping malls. I loved reading about the resurrection of inner cities, led by young urban pioneers, before "yuppie" was a bad word, or maybe even a word at all.

In Chicago once, I met a lawyer who worked for the National Trust. Soul mate, I thought. She said, I'm really an environmentalist, I don't really have a feeling for architecture. I was appalled. This was hard for me to understand. I told her over and over: You must see the Victorian Gothic apartments at Chicago and Wabash. The building is in danger. It is beautiful. It must be saved.

They say you'll see everybody you know if you stand long enough at the corner of State and Madison. I see Louis, that is all that matters. I am talking about a building. I am talking about Carson Pirie Scott designed by Louis Sullivan. The green and rust filigree ironwork. The design inspired by organic shapes, the same energy of nature that animated Whitman. This ersatz vegetation fills my heart, the way that Sullivan's first view of a suspension bridge shook him up as a boy. An exhilaration. The same feeling I get from walking down a certain street in my neighborhood, Roscoe—the pedestrian scale of the two-flats and three-flats, the undulation of the brick fronts, the Italianate eyebrows on windows, decorative carvings on graystones—the way *someone* must react to the undulations of corn, clouds, furrows.

Or the straight vastness of the Great Plains with their wheat, earth, sand, clay—whatever is on them, in them.

I liked *Charlotte's Web*—and it appears to have been a farm novel.

I fear the Other.

I am afraid nothing is out there but God and landscape, and he doesn't exist and land can't talk. I don't know the language of it.

I like crowded civic and political events during which everyone believes something important is happening.

We city folks go to therapy.
We fantasize about strangers on the el.
We fool ourselves into thinking we have a shared destination.
We fool ourselves into thinking we don't.

This is the secret, the secret I have always known: that the bare open plain is my heart itself, my heart without connection; that the bare cinderblock room is my soul, my soul without connection—the place I fear I will end up when the fear of loss of connection overrides everything else.

I long to receive this benediction: May you see that something is always there, have hope for the heart to rise up for, come to a feeling of settlement, find a light way of walking on the earth.

A City for Human-clams: a Plea for Environmental Immobility
LIAM HENEGHAN

A young man of my acquaintance, adequately nourished, and provided with a room and a gaming console appears to be sustainable, quite extraordinarily so, in the environmental sense. He has a small physical footprint. A few square feet of a pleasantly upholstered couch in an ill-lit room is all that is needed to sustain him. From this perch he can command vast legions of hobgoblins, medieval warlocks, sport heroes, and assorted heavily-armed movie characters. He can distract himself for days at a time, emerging from his room very occasionally, like a three-toed sloth, to pad to the latrine. An army of youth so employed needs little in the way of a great outdoors. Slightly soiled pajamas, or underpants, it seems, can suffice for clothing. The nutritional requirements of this battalion extend little beyond sodas and pop-tarts. In light of this, might it not be wise for us to reverse course, and rather than advocating strenuously, as many of us have, for urban kids to get out of doors to cultivate responsible environmental stewardship, *might we not instead council the cultivation of obsessive gameplay*, reclassifying it as environmentally laudable behavior?

If we take this pragmatic tack, setting aside our pious feelings about the "old environment" and the worthy pleasures to be found there, it is apparent that there are several tendencies in contemporary life that we might encourage rather than scorn. We have for too long decried our sedentary natures and the accompanying tendencies towards corpulence of body and spirit. Bloat a little, rest a little more; you are doing your bit for the environment. Applaud your small adventures in the *great indoors* – a peregrination from fridge to sofa will never have felt so good, and the lazy-boy is a fine environmental destination. Think of the gas saved compared with a trip to Yosemite – no planes, no trains, no automobiles. Even if your kids might like to romp in the corn fields of some distant rural hinterland, spare yourself the self-laceration. Quite simply a family ensconced in a moderately appointed metropolitan apartment may well have a smaller environmental cost than a family whizzing around in their so-called mini-van in some suburban Eden.

A back of the envelope calculation shows that the environmental footprint of the immobile is smaller that of one in constant auto-motion. Whole earths can be saved by *merely standing still*.

To add just another small suggestion: if we could just promote a little selective devolution – a stepping back in evolutionary time – this could be amply rewarding in terms of a greatly reduced human impact. Many successful organisms are rooted in one place! Rather than conveying themselves to their messy foodstuffs, (often, it should be noted, by means of a tedious and energetic bumbling, swinging, galloping or walking), *their food comes to them*. But let us not be guilty of absurdity in our aspirations: advocating a return to plant life would be foolishness and any half-meditative evolutionist would remind us that plants are exquisitely evolved organisms in their own right – there is no "going back" to plants. No, rather we should devolve to the condition of the sessile organisms: something like a sea anemone or a coral or a barnacle. In fact, any animal that fixes itself to a substrate and waits for food to come its way can serve as a model. Lest this seem implausible, it should be noted that the evolutionary mechanism to achieve this is available to us already. There is nothing new under the sun, we have been told. And indeed if we follow the simple edict of *switching our sexual fancies* to those of our species that are *already sluggish*, this should start paying evolutionary dividends fairly rapidly. The children of a union between a gamer, for instance, and let's say a knitter, or a pursuer of any of the meticulously slow-paced crafts (other excellent choices for biddable partners: scrapbookers, quilters, origami enthusiasts), should have sessile tendencies, on the basis of meticulous calculations ratified by the most rigorous of the sciences. It is hard to see why love-matches between pursuits that require nimble fingers rather than active legs should not provide an excellent evolutionary fresh start for the "new species" of human-kind.

As generation surpasses generation, human progeny should put down roots, so to speak; not, of course, as actual roots. No, plant roots are energetically expensive, diverting valuable resources from above to below. Rather, I advocate, indeed I predict, a simple anchoring of flesh to rock. We shall extrude byssal strands like our distant cousins amongst the molluscs. Imagine therefore entire villages or cities of human-clams, adhering firmly to bare rock, content to stay in one place, perhaps busily knitting, viewing television, or at play in sundry and sedentary ways.

Now you may object that this solution to our environmental problems, despite its initial attractiveness, is flawed in one crucial respect. Human need for nutriment may not be easily satisfied in this otherwise plausible scenario. One obvious solution is to train the lesser species, which otherwise do nothing particularly useful, to provision us with some necessary morsels. Would it really be difficult for a well-trained bonnet monkey to bake small treats (how difficult can it be to make a pop-tart) and to brew calorific beverages and serve them to their quiescent masters and mistresses? In India this species already pesters us; can we not harness their antrophilia for good? Adding to the charm of this solution, consider this: since *monkeys are part of nature*, their "environmental impacts", by definition, do not count as "environmental damage." (like earthquakes, volcanoes and marauding elephants, some seemingly enormous damage does not count at all!)

Remember finally that in current models of climate change sea levels are predicted to rise. Most of our coastal areas will be flooded. Where formerly this would have been an enormous human tragedy, under our new evolutionary regime it now, of course, seems like the final piece falling into place. Cities of pedunculate humans, heads bobbing freely like the smiling calyxes of large aquatic plants can then dispense with monkeys, and can wait for good and tasty sea-things to waft on by.

Drawings

PETER KARKLINS

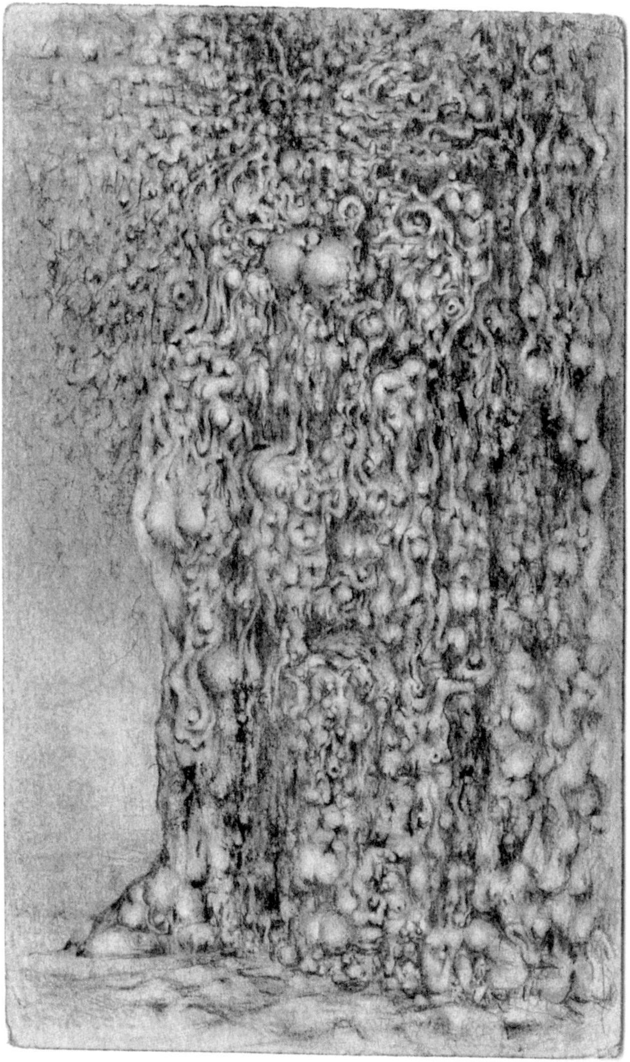

BRUTE NEIGHBORS

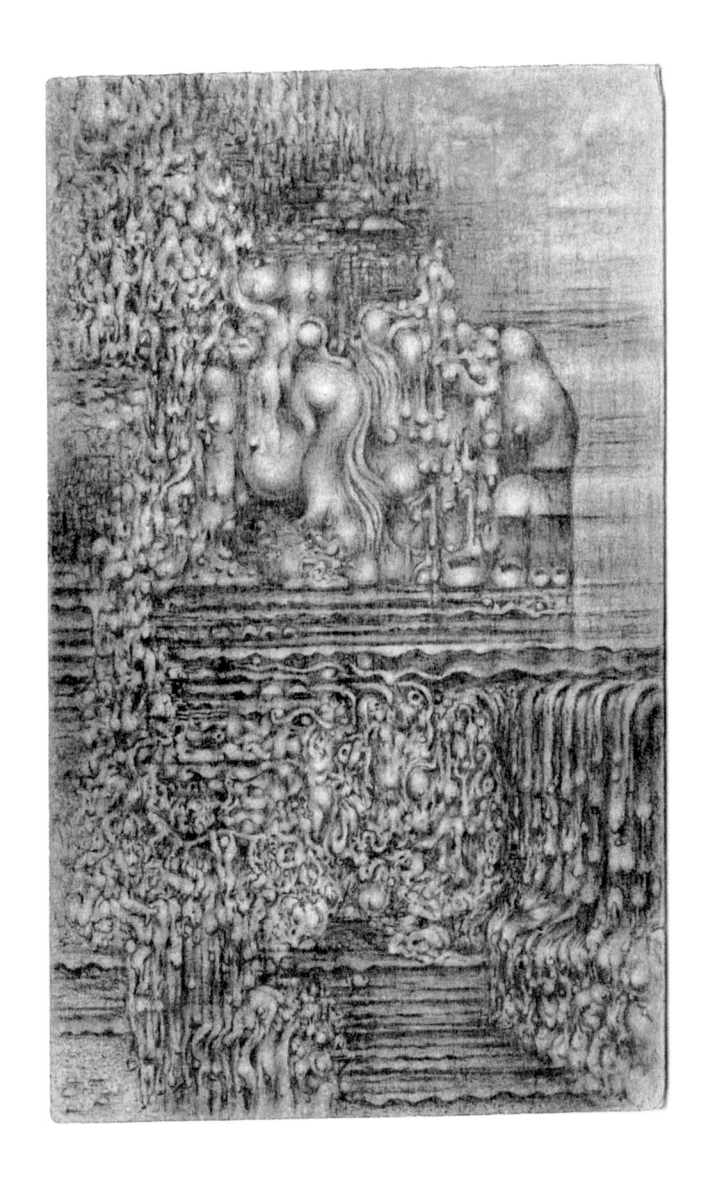

Archaic Nature   *SEAN D. KIRKLAND*

The thoughts expressed in this essay arose in response to a series of 48 small pencil drawings by the Chicago artist Peter Karklins, three of which are reproduced here. The artist himself has referred to these as "nature drawings," and I would suggest that we resist the temptation to dismiss them as fantastical and imaginary, as mere dreamscapes. Instead we might try to confront them as expressing a new and bizarre realism, a deeper naturalism. We might allow these works to present us with a vitally non-objective, disturbingly fertile, archaic Nature, one not set apart from the human, but emphatically intertwined with it. This will be a Nature that we stumble upon only within the artist's momentary suspension of our objectifying gaze, the gaze that still sets the parameters for thought and action in our late modern historical moment.

***

In caring for Nature, in addressing it as an object of concern, one's gaze is confined from the outset to precisely that which science finds beneath its instruments and which technology presses into the service of a human will. As we study, expose, and even strive to correct the ecological catastrophe that confronts us today, these very efforts indicate that no transformation has taken place in our most basic conception of Nature. That is, even if revalued or newly assessed, Nature remains an *ob-jectum*, something cast or thrown over against us, something placed in opposition to us. This is not at all to suggest the abandoning of urgent practical initiatives. However, we should allow ourselves the worrying suspicion that these remain triage measures that leave the underlying disease untouched. Hoping to intensify such a worry then, let us consider here the consequences of the objectifying modern view of Nature from which it seems so difficult to extricate ourselves.

An early and especially clear expression of this view is found in Descartes' 1637 *Discourse on Method*. Hoping to secure certain and scientific knowledge through the hyperbolic skeptical interrogation of all his sensations, opinions, and beliefs, Descartes' philosophy instead managed to open up a gap, a chasm between the subject and its object, the real external world or Nature. Indeed, the entire subsequent history of modern philosophy can be understood as a series of responses to this severance, attempting to secure certain knowledge of what is objectively real. Of course, in the *Discourse*, Descartes claims to be after more than merely theoretical truth in any case, more than idle speculation about the world. Rather, he hopes first and foremost to have a positive effect on human life. For Descartes, however, any such practical philosophy is understood to require "knowing the force and the actions of fire, water, air, the stars, the heavens, and all the other bodies that surround us, just as distinctly as we know the various skills of our craftsmen, so that we might be able, in the same way, to use them for all the purposes for which they are appropriate, and thus render ourselves, as it were, masters and possessors of nature." Thus, with Descartes, Nature emerges as an object situated over against an autonomous subject with its godlike will and this now objectified Nature presents itself immediately as *to be mastered, to be dominated*.

At the other end of the modern period, in 1930, we find this very same attitude still at work in Sigmund Freud's *Civilization and Its Discontents*. Freud first identifies three causes of pain or unpleasure for human beings—ourselves, one another, and the natural world. In negotiating these threats to our happiness, we must employ the reality principle, learning what can be expected and taking action on the basis of these expectations. We use various palliative measures to reduce the suffering imposed on us by our own bodies and by other human beings, but against "the dreaded external world" the first available response would seem to be that of complete withdrawal, taking shelter from the menacing storm that Freud takes Nature to be. However, Freud observes, "There is, indeed, another and better path: that of becoming a member of the human community, and, with the help of technique guided by science, going over to the attack against nature and subjecting her to the human will." Again, once we find ourselves set over against Nature as an object, we become instantly bloody minded. Despite the hell that is other people, we enter human society in order that, by marshalling our collective forces and directing them technologically and scientifically, we can undertake more elaborate and extended campaigns against our adversary, Nature.

The inescapable oppositional logic of objectivity having been indicated, we are left with the question of whether there is any other relation to Nature available to us today. Surely, any simple retrieval of a romantic attitude, some worshipful comportment toward a divinized nature, will seem hopelessly naïve in a scientific age such as ours. And as suggested above, even our sincere concern and our best reparative measures leave Nature untouched as that same object which, once opposed to us, is so quickly and so thoroughly reduced to raw material to be bent and molded according to every imaginable human caprice.

However, where there is danger, there also resides some saving power. Hölderlin assures us of this and Freud's text would seem to lend the claim some credence. For in the opening section of the *Civilization and Its Discontents*, Freud himself introduces an altogether different mode of relating to Nature and with it a different conception of Nature itself. To be sure, he declares this relation "infantile," proper only to the earliest stage of human development. According to Freud, human development entails a painful process of detaching one's ego from one's world. Immediately after birth, there exists "a much more intimate bond between the ego and the world around it." Indeed, "originally the ego includes everything." A distinction is introduced between the infant and the external world only once the infant's desire fails to be immediately gratified, i.e. when the world puts up resistance. Freud then connects this infantile stage with what he discusses as an "oceanic feeling," a feeling of eternity or boundlessness that his friend Romain Rolland had suggested to Freud was the seed of all religiosity.

Despite Freud's dismissing this feeling as "pathological" among adult human beings, it would seem that, if it could be provoked, if *this* relation to Nature could be uncovered even momentarily, some trace of the Nature it entails might remain. It might then be possible to think Nature otherwise, no longer reducing it to an object. Indeed, this non-objective Nature, in relation to which we suffer no Cartesian separation, seems to be precisely what the archaic, pre-Socratic Greek philosophers thought as '*phusis*.' Although this term (from which we derive our 'physics') is usually rendered into English simply as 'nature,' its connection to the verb '*phuein*,' meaning 'to emerge, unfold, burgeon forth,' encourages us to find in it an essentially dynamic and emergent movement. This would be a Nature experienced as the active *fons et origo* not only of the world that bursts forth and presents itself to us, but of us as well. A Nature experienced from within. No adversarial object at all, it would be understood first as an essentially dynamic process of emergence into existence whereby the world of individual beings unfolds itself into view before us even as we are constituted as that world's thoughtful recipients.

Experiencing this unknown or, perhaps better, forgotten Nature, this underlying and self-concealing dynamism that joins us to the world, is a question of violently disturbing our objectifying gaze. No doubt, deep and widespread alterations in the actual treatment of our environment are urgently needed, for tomorrow promises disaster in no uncertain terms. But provided that we can make a tomorrow possible with immediate and real practical remedies, we must ultimately change more than our behavior. And this seems to require first not a concerned defense or study of Nature, but a deregulation at the most fundamental level of our orthodox sense of Nature, our experience of it. Only thus, in the breakdown of our familiarly intelligible notion, might we encounter Nature as an archaic originating power still hidden and preserved beneath our present world of natural objects.

Old Airs

PERRY A. ZURN

I brushed past my doorstep – fumbling to drop my keys in my pack, slide my wallet in my right back pocket, and straighten my tie – when it hit me. It was the kind of breeze that stills you in your tracks, drop-kicks your eyelids, and gives you wings. *I know you*, I thought: Hertzler Drive, at the foot of Twin Valley Road, just beyond the cornfield and across from the wheat. But I am not in no-man's-land Pennsylvania; I am in the heart of North Chicago, on Broadway Avenue. *What are you doing here?*

I instinctively associate a proper breeze with what lies outside the city: vast stretches of land, striated by unpaved roads and speckled, if at all, with long, low buildings – as if any breeze worthy of the name blows over what is bare. But, a breeze seems to require even less: total non-existence. For, its apparently impeccable pedigree begins right at the beginning when, as Genesis 1:2 so memorably states, "The earth was without form and void; darkness was upon the face of the deep. And the Spirit of God moved upon the face of the waters" (KJV). The Vulgate's *spiritus* translates the Hebrew *ruah*, meaning breath, air, or wind. It is a breeze, then – or a wind in the space of a breath – that first flutters over darkness, over absence – beyond the city and behind humankind – uninterrupted, free. Or at least that's one story.

Not every account of wind consigns it to The Nothing and blames it for the advent of everything. Take the Milesian School in the 6th century BC, for instance. Thales said all reality was composed of water, Anaximander suggested it was 'boundless stuff' (*apeiron*), but Anaximenes argued that the sum total of existence could be explained as some form of air (*aer*). The Greeks distinguished between *aer* and *aither*, the low wind and high: the latter is dry and feathery, while the first is stringy and wet. For Anaximenes, *aer* is the mist, vapor, or general troposphere which rarefies into fire or condenses into dirt and stone. Air is like fine wool, he mused: it can be fluffed up and sprinkled about or flattened and compressed into felt. From his vantage point, this whole urban jungle is but a discarded cap – the mere felt remnant of a breeze.

Down the corridors of time, the wind has hardly settled well as either an inhabitant of The Nothing or the habitat for everything. You remember, of course, the Hippocratic Oath. Well, one of its companions is Hippocrates' treatise *Peri Physon*. While it was long ago translated into the Latin, rather closely, as *De Flatibus*, its English title wiggles and wafts a bit, across the centuries: *The Winds* here, just *Breaths* there, and sometimes the boldly indecorous *On Flatulence*. But the sense of the manuscript is quite steady: both health and disease supervene on the movement of inner airs. Hippocrates essentially proposes that life and death, creation and annihilation, require an air that is paradoxically free within the confines of things. This air may even be the sort breathed into the blowhole of a wind instrument, as the Greek title suggests.

Whatever his personal relationship to natural gases, Hippocrates may have been on to more than he knew. For Saint Augustine, the flurry of a fife is but an instance in a long typological sequence. In *On Christian Doctrine*, Augustine marks that the gesture, the musical note, and the word share one thing in common: funneled *spiritus*. In *The Trinity*, he takes it one step further, "Our word is so made in some way into an articulate sound of the body [...] as the Word of God was made flesh, by assuming that flesh in which itself also might be manifested to men's senses" (*XV*). The human spirit in a gesticulating body, animal breath in a wooden instrument, a word pronounced through lips and teeth, God made flesh – in each case, the intangible air passes through tangible things to form a signal, to communicate, to make meaning.

The press of all these old airs can be suffocating, or they can realize that of which they sing. I imagine Chicago as a site of fasciculate incarnation. I see in Willis Tower the condensed howls of winter. I can suddenly make some sense of Chicago's healthy mythology as the Windy City – a little blustery, a little bombast, lots of air and a little hot air: flatulent self-flattery. Or at last, I settle into a favored line of imagery –the city of Chicago as a monstrous mouth gaping 22 miles wide, with serrated teeth guarding its throat and Tasset's eyeball caught at the back. In this scenario, perhaps my baby breeze is just Chicago readying to say a word it rarely says. Its mouth is poised – whether to utter something soft or sinister, *nescio*: I cannot tell – which is perhaps why it halted me a moment, and got my attention. I listen.

A Garden in Eden BARBARA WILLARD
PHOTOGRAPHS BY RANDALL HONOLD

In July 2010 I went off to the "urban jungle" to discover how gardeners have reshaped communities by transforming the land: I went off to find hope in a garden. Of the 41 homicides in Chicago that month, most occurred in the neighborhoods I visited. Still, I wondered as I drove by the empty lots, plywood-covered windows, a crack house, and failed businesses if nature could exist in this urban blight. I wondered, alongside formidable social theorist Henri Lefebvre, if a community could really create an inspiring message about their place in this city, and if they could do this by renewing their relationship with the natural world.

What I found was Eden Place, formerly an illegal dumping ground in Chicago's urban wasteland, today a remarkable scene of restored natural beauty. Further down the Dan Ryan expressway I stumbled upon the Artists' Garden, spread out over four vacant lots. Both gardens operate outside of the urban blight and challenge crime and environmental pollution by demonstrating there is more to their neighborhoods than bleak statistics imply. The gardens invite residents to think of other ways of being, other ways of expression, in their community. These gardens ask people to peacefully and harmoniously co-exist with other life forms (and by implication, other people). In the past decade cities across the US have witnessed a growth in these unconventional sites of nature–community gardens where nature and culture blend together testifying to the strong bond between humans and the land.

Fuller Park is just north of Englewood, the most violent and dangerous community in Chicago. It is a "food desert," a place where large grocery chains are scarce and residents have little access to fresh produce. It is far easier to find a bag of chips and a pack of smokes at the corner convenience store than a fresh apple and a head of lettuce. In this unlikely place, Michael Howard, a long-time resident and community activist, created a nature center on a three-and-a-half-acre site sandwiched between an alley and a raised railroad track heavily traveled by trains hauling freight to the inner city. With the help of his wife and five children, he organized the neighbors to move over 200 tons of debris from the lot and planted a garden. This year they opened the Eden Place Farmers Market where neighbors can purchase locally grown fruit and vegetables throughout the growing season.

After years of layoffs during the downfall of the steel industry, US Steel finally shut its doors in 1992, leaving behind 576 abandoned acres, a host of unemployed workers and an economically depressed community. A few blocks away from the old US Steel site is the Artists' Garden.

I got a personal tour from one of the community gardeners, Miguel, a Mexican immigrant who lives adjacent to the Artists' Garden. A rooster crows from one of the nearby 25 community plots. It belongs to "Crazy Hat" whose garden is across the alleyway. An adobe oven, a flock of chickens, and beehives populate Crazy Hat's garden. Miguel notices that one beehive is too high in the tree. Full of surprising rustic wisdom, he tells me that in this circumstance the bees will "become confused" and unable to thrive. He excuses himself to fetch a ladder so he can move the beehive lower to the ground.

On this quest, the most improbable circumstances—a garden in Eden, Mr. Howard's Farmers Market, and a flock of chickens in the shadows of a shuttered steel mill.

* The former Rich's Food Mart represents layers of food insecurity. Where once residents could find "frozen food, candy, and chips" now there is only boarded up windows.
* The photo of "Mr. Green Jeans" is Greg Bratton – a leader in the urban agriculture and community gardening movement in Chicago. His passion is "to feed people and keep them safe." He farms with a variety of organizations including Growing Power.
* The ruins of a former housing project form the backdrop for fields of lettuce at City Farms in downtown Chicago.
*Gourds were spread throughout the world as humans migrated. These iconic fruits form the threshold of the community gathering spot for Mexican immigrants in the Artists' Garden.

Turf

ELIZABETH CRANE

The story you are about to hear is made up and the reason it's made up is because we don't know the half of it. But just in case it seems familiar, rest assured that names, places and details are made up too. This story takes place in the large Midwestern city of Hicago, which as you are surely aware, does not even exist, much of it not existing at a dog park very close to the intersection of Hackhawk and Heaver, which is also made up. So there should be no concern, we think, about anyone's feelings getting hurt, or any misunderstandings or what have you.

The two main characters here are the dog walker Hulie and the dog owner Helizabeth.

Hulie, we're pretty sure, has lived on that block her whole life. She's maybe twenty-six. Twenty-six years ago that block was rough. Ten years ago that block was rough. Now there are some condos, but sometimes in the mornings we'll see so much shattered glass by the curb, we wonder about the window-smashing spree the night before, who around here thinks that's a good time. We don't have suspicions, but we think Hulie might. We also think it's completely possible that she's never been on a plane.

Helizabeth has lived on Heaver Street for about five years now. More is known, factually, about Helizabeth than Hulie because Helizabeth is a local author and you can google her just like she does. Plus she's on Hacebook and Hyspace and blogs and all that. Hulie doesn't even go online, we'd say. So anyway Helizabeth and her then-boyfriend-now-husband Hen moved in there together, got married a few months later in the backyard. Last year, having postponed making the baby decision for a while, Helizabeth and Hen decided it was time to get a dog, and a sweet stray found its way to them through a friend at the Hatahoula Rescue, and Helizabeth and Hen brought home their new baby, a sickly fifty-pound ten-month-old with a soft gray coat covered with the trademark Hatahoula purple, pink and white markings. They named him Herky.

Initially, Herky was a mellow dog, awkward in social settings, no way was he alpha, he wasn't even beta he was more like mu or nu or romichon, way into the second half of the Greek alphabet. At the dog park, Herky would make efforts to play, wagging his butt and bouncing around in that puppy way, but inevitably, after annoying one of the alphas with his eager doggy dorkiness, he'd end up pushed into a corner. Herky was not one of the cool kids.

But over the year, Herky gained a few pounds along with some confidence, and although he still never became alpha he for sure moved up to maybe around theta. He still isn't much interested in bossing anyone around, and will never start a fight, but if you do, he will defend himself.

What we actually know about Hulie: She has a Great Hane named Hurphy. Around noon every day, she arrives at the dog park with a minivan full of barking dogs, stays there for a couple of hours. Every so often, she'll throw a well-chewed ball for them, but calling this game *fetch* would be a stretch because it tends to be a long time between throws, and we've never one time witnessed her showing affection to a dog. Not one time. She appears to know a lot of folks in the immediate vicinity, and will frequently engage in lengthy conversations with them. Words and phrases we overhear in these conversations regularly include *terrible*, *I'm not*, and *they never*. Hulie doesn't smile much, in these conversations, or ever. Hulie yells at her dogs a lot and we've also seen her hit them. The police have come around to see her, but not because of that. What Hulie does, bringing the dogs to the park, isn't really legal, but because she seems to know so many folks, it seems that someone in the 'hood is looking out for her. There's an ex-congressman on the block and we've seen them chatting.

What we think we know about Hulie: Her boyfriend Hoger lives downstairs from her. It's possible that they live together, but probably not. Our best guess is that they met in the laundry room. Her apartment is sparsely decorated, if the word *decorated* is even appropriate. She'd like it to be a little nicer, but just doesn't know how to go about it, doesn't really have the time. There are a couple of pictures hung in odd locations, too high or low, no doubt on nails that were already in the walls. There's a spider plant in a macramé hanger by the window, but lately it doesn't look too good. Sometimes at Walgreen's she'll pick up a scented Glade candle. Her sofa is a futon in a frame; on it is an earth-toned afghan she thinks her grandmother crocheted, but it isn't true. That was a story her mother told her. No one knows who made it. Hulie doesn't cook much, will get a roasted chicken or a salad at the Jewel, maybe something frozen from Aldi but that's a little too far down Hilwaukee and she's not over that way too much. Once a year her boyfriend will take her to some fancy sushi place like Haponais, because he heard celebrities go there. But she won't really be impressed, and she won't really like it. She will order something cooked.

Her bedroom is more or less the same. She sleeps on a mattress on the floor and there's a large pile of laundry in the corner. Hurphy isn't allowed to sleep in the bed, but since her bed is close to the floor, Hurphy sleeps right next to her on the nights when Hoger isn't over. When Hoger is over Hurphy sleeps in the living room because Hoger doesn't like the dog watching them fuck. Hoger's words.

In her bathroom, Hulie's bikini panties are strewn about, the kind that have words on the butt in big letters, words like SEXY or HOTT. This is about as girly as she gets, really she's kind of a tomboy, but she uses Suave Juicy Green Apple shampoo, there's a curling iron on the sink, and on New Year's Eve you saw her walking Hurphy in a long black jersey gown under her fleece jacket. She may have also been wearing blush.

When she's not hanging out with Hoger, once in a while she'll watch those home improvement shows where people come in and fix up a room for under a thousand dollars, and thinks how nice it would be to have someone do that for her. The last book she read was *Men Are from Mars, Women Are from Venus* which her sister had sent her from Arizona (she'd gotten the fuck out of the neighborhood and all the way out of the state as soon as she graduated high school), but she didn't finish it because it was a bunch of horseshit she already knew anyhow and Hulie wasn't likely to take her sister's advice on romance seeing as how she was married to a blazing asshole. Hulie's sister is twelve years older, but there were never very close even in that almost-parent sisterly kind of way. Hulie does not have a group of girlfriends, does not have a girlfriend, has not had a girlfriend since her childhood friend Hennifer totally made out with her boyfriend Hichie right in front of her face at her own thirteenth birthday party. Hennifer had tried to point out that in kissing games you kiss, but Hulie wasn't having it. Mostly, in her spare time, Hulie does Sudoku or hangs around out front with whoever's playing cornhole.

So Hulie dates Hoger, and she works with dogs but she doesn't smile. How does someone work with dogs and not smile, like, constantly? We wonder if somebody hit her. If we weren't so sure she's been on this block since forever, we'd wonder if she was one of those foster kids you hear about who gets moved sixteen times and hit in fifteen of them. We wonder if someone hit her somewhere along the line because we can't come up with any other reason why someone who works with dogs would just never smile. We hope it wasn't Hoger, but we could believe it. Or maybe in ninth grade she was on color guard and kind of liked it and would defend it as totally being a sport but skipped it one afternoon to meet a cute druggy boy behind the physical plant and never went back because he said it was way lame and she spent the next two years alternating between doing it with him in his garage and getting hit by him if she wasn't in the mood or if she had her period. Probably, she wanted to be something once, but she forgot what.

What little we know about Hoger: Hoger has a great head of hair but he seems to favor an old-school heavy Brylcreem look, slicked straight back, very Gordon Gekko. He wears a suit to work (maybe at the Hoard of Trade?), some designer suit that he paid a thousand dollars for so he can tell people it's Hugo Boss except after he got it off the rack he never took it to get tailored and so it doesn't fit quite right. Okay, I guess we don't know that for sure but that's what it looks like. We do know that he has a Hottweiler named Hex and that when he brings Hex to the dog park he stays for about the length of a smoke or until Hex *makes*, Hoger's word, whichever comes first. We suspect Hoger isn't one to really decorate either, but we are completely sure he has that framed poster of naked Nastassja Kinski with the snake. Never mind that it's before his era. He saw it on sale at a dollar store for $5.99 and his mind was blown. Hulie doesn't care for it one bit, but Hoger won't budge. He tells her when she poses naked with a snake he'll take it down. She tells him he can fuck Nastassja Kinski until that day and he says *You think I couldn't hit that?* And she says *Whatever, she's like fifty now anyways, go ahead.*

Helizabeth and Hen's apartment is a rental and it's big and old and perpetually dusty but it's filled with books and art, real art; Hen is an artist. Helizabeth makes books. They don't have tons of money or anything, but they have some nice pieces of furniture and Helizabeth makes curtains and pillows and it feels like a home. Hen built a bed for Herky. They too have a laundry pile, but Helizabeth tries her best to make sure it stays in the closet. They drink loose tea and grind their coffee and are working on going organic and weaning off high-fructose corn syrup, if it weren't for the problem of things like Hunky Monkey ice cream being so good. They shop mostly at Trader Hoe's but if they have a little extra cash some week they'll splurge at Hole Foods.

Okay, so now we'll finally move on to the story part of the story.
One morning, Helizabeth took Herky out for his morning walk–Hen is on mornings most days, but it was a holiday and those are usually Helizabeth's. Herky and Helizabeth were playing fetch when Hulie came in with Hurphy and Hex and another dog. Helizabeth and Hulie had a brief conversation but perhaps the longest they'd ever had. Something like *Hey. Hey. Dust from the construction is terrible, huh? Awful, yeah. I cleaned up a ton of their garbage, too. They never clean it up. I'm always doing that. Yeah, I had to tell a guy to put his beer bottles in the trash. What guy? I dunno, some guy that told me he lives right over here. I know that guy, he doesn't live there. I heard he got his girlfriend pregnant and she doesn't want anything to do with him so he comes out here to drink. Oh. I know, can you believe it? I've told him so many times... Are you dog sitting this weekend? Story of my life.* Hulie says it like it's a perpetual drag, this thing she chose to do for a living. Still, Helizabeth, we guess, feels bad for judging Hulie so harshly because Hulie's sadness is so obvious, and sees a small window where maybe they'll have a conversation in the positive someday, maybe chat about *Grey's Anatomy* or Britney Spears or something.

Something else that is known by all parties: Hex is a ball hog. You pretty much can't have Hex and a ball in the park together if you're interested in holding onto that ball. If Hex gets the ball, the ball belongs to Hex. Otherwise, Hex is pretty agreeable as dogs go. Usually, Helizabeth will take the ball away from Herky when Hex comes in, but in this case, waited until it was too late, and an incident occurred.

There are differences of opinion about the specifics of this incident, but the result was that Herky, no longer a shy, sickly puppy, emboldened by his health and new robustness, decided not to allow the taking of the ball, and a brief dogfight occurred. Helizabeth and Hulie broke the fight up quickly, but not before Hex left with a cut on his lip and Herky left with a small but deep gash in his side.

Helizabeth's solution to this problem was to avoid the dog park around lunchtime.

A couple of weeks went by and Helizabeth was at the park with Herky around 11 am when Hulie was leaving to pick up her dogs. What we could make of it: Hulie came over and tried to start a conversation about it. Something like, *Listen, I'm hearing that you're going around saying Hex attacked your dog and that's not what happened.* Helizabeth said something like *Where did you hear that* and Hulie said *Dog park gossip*, and Helizabeth said *Well I never said attacked, I said bit*, and Hulie said *But why were you even talking about it* and Helizabeth said *Look at that gash, people were asking, even the vet was like Whoa, what happened here* and Hulie said *You didn't have to take him to the vet*, and Helizabeth said *What?* And Hulie said *Did he get stitches?* And Helizabeth said *No* and Hulie said *Then you didn't need to go to the vet* and Helizabeth, getting to that point in the argument where you start defending yourself by making lists, she said *Okay, A) we didn't know if he needed stitches or not, and B) who are you to tell me whether I should take my dog to the vet*, and Hulie said *I see it all the time, dogs get cut up, it's no big deal*, Helizabeth said *Okay, whatever, this has nothing to do with anything*, and Hulie said *Anyways I just didn't like what I heard*, and Helizabeth said, *Well I told you the truth*, and Hulie said *But that's not what I heard what I heard was attacked*, and this attacked vs. bit thing went around a few more times and Helizabeth said *Look, I can't make you believe me* and then at this point there was a rehashing of the incident, Hulie said that Herky started it and Helizabeth said *No, Herky growled as if to warn Hex off, and then Hex went after Herky*, and Hulie said *That's not true because you had your back turned, you don't even know*, and Helizabeth at this point was starting to lose it, and we've never seen her like this before, although it's not unbelievable, we imagine her as the sort of person who can remain calm through quite a number of circumstances way worse than a fight at the dog park, but then will reach a point where she begins to lose it, and this was that point, and Helizabeth raised up her arms dramatically and said *Are you joking me? I was facing you, we were talking, and the dogs were between us* and Hulie said *Well I don't know* and Helizabeth said *Well I know! I know!* and Hulie also said *Hex is a nice dog but a lot of people are saying they don't want to come in here when Herky's here*, and Helizabeth said *WHAT, WHAT, who, who are these a lot of people*, and Hulie named a dog and Helizabeth said *Herky and that dog were friends until he started a fight with Herky, and his mom knows that*, and Hulie said *Well I'm just telling you what I hear, that a lot of people are afraid of Herky* and Helizabeth said *Who else?* And Hulie, whose unaffected demeanor only served to further raise Helizabeth's hackles, named this other dog and Helizabeth said *That is the most ill-mannered dog whose parents have no control over him whatsoever, and he harasses Herky, not the other way around and those people know it too. Everyone leaves the park when that dog comes in*. And Hulie said *Well I'm just telling you what I hear* and Helizabeth said *Who else* and Hulie said *Well that's all I know* and Helizabeth said *Well that's two dogs which isn't a lot especially since it's them and not Herky so I don't see how that's a lot, actually I don't see how that's any, especially considering I heard your boyfriend bragged about Hex eating a puppy for lunch*. Which at that moment was arguably neither here nor there, we had the impression that this was a point Helizabeth might have used more effectively at a different point in her argument. Hulie told her *If he did say that I'm sure it was a joke* and Helizabeth said that that wasn't the impression she had and Hulie said *Well I don't know alls I know is there's a lot of gossip and I don't want anyone to feel uncomfortable or like whoever wants to come here can't come here*. And at this point Helizabeth appeared to be at a loss for words but finally said *Well, I feel like it's understood that this is your corner*, and Hulie said *Well I'm sorry if I gave you that impression, did I give you that impression?* and Helizabeth said *I don't know if you gave it to me but that's the impression I have* and Hulie said *Well I'm sorry about that, I don't want to give that impression* and Helizabeth shrugged like she thought Hulie really did want to give that impression and said *Well it's just a little intimidating* and Hulie said *Well that's too bad*, like she meant it, like she was genuinely implying that it was too bad that Helizabeth felt too intimidated to come back to the park but that she'd probably get over it fast enough even though just that holiday morning, before the incident, our guess is that Hulie had started to turn a corner on Helizabeth, thinking maybe she wasn't so bad. It seemed to us like in that moment they both knew the other wasn't so bad but that they'd had their shot and it was over. We also speculate that Hulie, still stung by the junior-high make-out debacle with Hennifer, was less surprised than mildly disappointed, and that Helizabeth still thought she was better than Hulie anyway. This may seem like all of it except in reality it went on for nearly an hour and also it was about seventeen degrees outside at the time.

What was learned? Immediately after the incident, Helizabeth thought it was a strong indicator that it was time to leave Hicago or at least to move off the block.

We speculate that Helizabeth and Hulie both had long conversations with their significant others, maybe more than one, and that Hoger and Hen both stood by their women, and that requests were put in by both women that the other not be mentioned again unless they were prepared for an argument, rational or otherwise. All we know for sure is that Helizabeth doesn't go to the park at noon anymore and Hulie still doesn't smile.

There's a lady on the block, a little old lady in a head scarf who every day gives bread to the birds and the cats and dogs. This seems to be her genuine joy and we don't want to take this away from her. We call her the bread lady and she always smiles, always. But she doesn't know anything for sure either.

ACKNOWLEDGMENTS

"Hungry" is reprinted from *Never-Ending Birds* by David Baker. Reprinted with permission of author. Published by Norton, 2009.

"Birds of Paradise" is reprinted from *Ice, Mouth, Song* by Rachel Contreni Flynn. Reprinted with permission of author. Published by Tupelo Press, 2005. This poem was first published in *Spillway*.

"Rising for the Buddha" is reprinted from *Apples of the Earth* by Dina Elenbogen. Reprinted with permission of author. Published by Spuyten Duyvil, NY 2006.

"Affect of Elms" is reprinted from *Sparrow: New & Selected Poems* by Reginald Gibbons. Reprinted with permission of Louisiana University Press.

"Deer Sonnets" is reprinted from *Epiphany School* by Chris Green. Reprinted with permission of author. Published by Mayapple Press, 2009. This poem was first published in *Black Clock*.

"July as a 1950's Sci Fi Movie" by Susen James was first published in *New American Writing*, 2001.

"Entering Strange Cities" by Alan Johnston was first published by the *Midwest Quarterly*, 2002.

"The House in Plano" is reprinted from *Harriet Rubin's Mother's Wooden Hand* by Susan Hahn. Reprinted with permission of author. Published by The University of Chicago Press, 1991.

"17-Year Itch" by Miles Harvey was first published by *Another Chicago Magazine*, number 50, volume 1.

"Summer Surprised Us" is reprinted from *Earthly Measures* by Ed Hirsch. Reprinted with permission of author. Published by Alfred A. Knopf, 1994.

"In This Hour," "Moon's/Flying," and "A Slow": grateful acknowledgment is made for permission to reprint text from: *Grasses Standing* by Ralph Mills Jr., Copyright 2000 by Ralph Mills Jr.

"Storm Lessons" by Patricia Monaghan was first published in *ISLE*.

"Windy City" is reprinted from *Restoration* by Christina Pugh. Reprinted with permission of author. Published by TriQuarterly Books/Northwestern University Press, 2008. This poem was first published in *Crab Orchard Review*, 2005.

"Torque" is reprinted from *Little Ice Age* by Maureen Seaton. Reprinted with permission of author. Published by Invisible Cities Press, 2001.

"High Holidays" by Don Share is forthcoming in *The Common* (Amherst College). Printed with permission of author.

"DED (Dutch Elm Disease)" by Don Share was first published on the *Verse* website. Reprinted with permission of author.

"Mechanical Foliage" is reprinted from *Star in the Eye* by James Shea. Reprinted with permission of Fence Books.

"Tree of Heaven" is reprinted from *The New Tenants* by Barry Silesky. Reprinted with permission of author.

"Small Boy" is reprinted from *Crowdpleaser* by Marc Smith. Reprinted with permission of author. Published by Collage Press, 1996.

"In the Intersection, Jackson and State" is reprinted from *The Lama's English Lessons* by Tony Trigilio. Reprinted with permission of author. Published by Three Candles Press, 2006.

"Tiny Moon Notebook" is reprinted from *Tiny Moon Notebook* (a chapbook) by David Trinidad. Reprinted with permission of author. Published by Big Game Books, 2007.

"Plain Scared, or: There Is No Such Thing as Negative Space, the Art Teacher Said" reprinted from *Holocaust Girls: History, Memory, and Other Obsessions* by S.L. Wisenberg by permission of the University of Nebraska Press. Copyright 2002 by the University of Nebraska Press.

"It Takes Particular Clicks" by Christian Wiman is forthcoming in *Every Riven Thing* (Farrar, Straus and Giroux). First published in *Slate*, 2009. Reprinted with permission of author.

BIOS

David Baker is author or editor of thirteen books of poetry and poetry criticism, most recently *Never-Ending Birds* (poems, W. W. Norton, 2009) and *Radiant Lyre: Essays on Lyric Poetry* (Graywolf, 2007). His poems appear widely in magazines here and abroad. Raised in Missouri, a life-long Midwesterner, he has lived in Granville, Ohio, for the past twenty-five years where he is Professor of English at Denison University and where he also serves as Poetry Editor of *The Kenyon Review*.

Virginia Bell's poetry has appeared in *A Writers' Congress: Chicago Poets on Barack Obama's Inauguration*, Woman Made Gallery's 2009 *Her Mark* date book, *Ekphrasis, Contrary Magazine,* and *Beltway Poetry Quarterly*, and is forthcoming in *Pebble Lake Review* (along with an audio version on PLR's web site). She is an associate editor of *RHINO* and an adjunct professor at Loyola University. Bell has a Ph.D. in Comparative Literature and has also published scholarly articles on activist writers such as Eduardo Galeano and Leslie Marmon Silko, as well the *Instructor's Resource Manual* for *Beyond Borders: A*

Cultural Reader (Houghton Mifflin, 2003).

Jan Bottiglieri lives in Schaumburg, Illinois with her husband and son. She is a freelance writer/editor and an editor for the poetry annual *RHINO*. Jan is pursuing her MFA in poetry from Pacific University; recent publications include poems in *Court Green*, *Margie*, *After Hours*, and the *Best of the Bellevue Literary Review* anthology. Growing up, a favorite urban nature encounter was visiting the Elk Grove Village elk grove every Thanksgiving to push saltines through the chain link fence to the thankful elk.

Kristy Bowen is the author of *in the bird museum* (Dusie Press, 2008) and *the fever almanac* (Ghost Road Press, 2006). She lives in Chicago, where she runs dancing girl press & studio, an indie press and design studio which publishes an annual chapbook series devoted to women poets , as well as the online lit zine *wicked alice*.

Margaret Brady, a recovering Catholic, journalist, and PR flack, received her MFA in Creative Writing/Poetry at Columbia College Chicago in 2007. Her work has appeared in *Court Green, Columbia Poetry Review, MiPoesias, Whistling Shade,* and *Rambunctious Review*. She also has a haiku at the Harrison "L" stop in Chicago. Margaret has been a featured reader at the Printers Row Book Fair in Chicago and at the *Rhino* magazine reading series in Evanston. She is the "token poet" member of the Union Street Gallery Collaborative Arts Guild, based in Chicago Heights, IL.

Brenda Cárdenas' collection of poetry *Boomerang* was published by Bilingual Review Press in 2009, and her chapbook *From the Tongues of Brick and Stone* by Momotombo Press (Institute for Latino/a Studies) in 2005. She also co-edited *Between the Heart and the Land: Latina Poets in the Midwest* (MARCH/Abrazo Press, 2001). Cardenas' work has appeared in a range of publications, including *Achiote Seeds, The City Visible: Chicago Poetry for the New Century, The Wind Shifts: The New Latino Poetry*, *RATTLE*, and the *Poetry Daily* website, among others. Her poem "Song" was recently made into an animated film in the *Poetry Everywhere* series sponsored by the Poetry Foundation. Cardenas is an Assistant Professor in the Creative Writing program at the University of Wisconsin-Milwaukee and is the 2010-2012 Milwaukee Poet Laureate.

Rachel Contreni Flynn's second full-length collection, *Tongue*, won the Benjamin Saltman Award and was published in 2010 by Red Hen Press. Her chapbook, *Haywire*, was published by Bright Hill Press in 2009. Her first book, *Ice, Mouth, Song*, was published in 2005 by Tupelo Press, after winning the Dorset Prize. She was awarded a Fellowship from the National Endowment for the Arts in 2007. Her work has twice been nominated for a Pushcart Prize, and she received an Illinois Arts Council Artists Fellowship in 2003. She is a graduate of the Warren Wilson College MFA Program and lives north of Chicago with her husband and two children.

Elizabeth Crane is the author of three collections of short stories, *When the Messenger is Hot*, *All this Heavenly Glory*, and *You Must Be This Happy to Enter*. Her work has also been featured in numerous publications, anthologies and on NPR's Selected Shorts. She is a recipient of the Chicago Public Library 21st Century Award, and her work has been adapted for the stage by Chicago's Steppenwolf Theater company, and has also been adapted for film. She currently teaches at UCR Palm Desert's Low Residency MFA program.

Helen Degen Cohen (Halina Degenfisz) received the NEA in poetry, 1st Prize in Britain's *Stand Magazine*, and three Illinois Arts Council Literary Awards. She's served as Illinois Artist-In-Education, taught for Roosevelt University, and co-founded and co-edits *Rhino*. She published two collections in 2009: *Habry*, and *On A Good Day One Discovers Another Poet*.

Mark Curran is an artist and educator who lives and works in Berlin and Dublin. Presently completing a PhD through the Centre for Transcultural Research and Media Practice, DIT, Dublin, he also lectures in the BA

(Hons) Photography programme at IADT, Dublin. Incorporating multimedia installation informed by ethnographic understandings, Curran's practice presently focuses upon the role and representation of labour, community and physical landscape in the predatory context of migrations of global capital. His first long-term project, SOUTHERN CROSS (Gallery of Photography, Dublin 2002), was widely published and exhibited and The Breathing Factory (Edition Braus/Belfast Exposed Photography 2006), the outcome of his doctoral research has been extensively presented internationally.

Mary Jane Duffy holds an MFA in painting and drawing from Northwestern University. She has exhibited her work in the U.S. and Mexico, including "Operation Human Intelligence" at Hyde Park Art Center in 2003, and "Color Key" at The Painting Center in New York City in 2008. Recent one-person exhibitions include "Sparkle" at Masmedula Galerie in Mexico City and "Shimmer/Shine" at Flatfile Galleries in 2006. She has received three CAAP grants from the Department of Cultural Affairs in Chicago and a Special Assistance Grant from the Illinois Arts Council. Since 1997 she has been teaching in the Fine Arts and First Year Programs at DePaul University.

Stuart Dybek is the author of two books of poetry and three books of fiction. His most recent book of poems, *Streets in Their Own Ink* (FSG), appeared in 2005. He is currently Distinguished Writer in Residence at Northwestern University.

Dina Elenbogen is the author of the poetry collection *Apples of the Earth* (Spuyten Duyvil, 2006). She recently completed a book-length memoir about her work with Ethiopian immigrants in Israel. Her writing has appeared in literary magazines including *Priairie Schooner*, *Rhino*, *Tikkun*, *Bellevue Literary Review* and in numerous anthologies. She is working on a second poetry collection and has new poetry forthcoming in *Paterson Literary Review* and *Zeek*. She has won fellowships from the Illinois Arts Council and his been nominated for a 2010 Pushcart. She teaches creative writing at the University of Chicago's Writer's Studio and lives in Evanston, Illinois where she communes with nature whenever she can.

Alice George's first collection—*This Must Be The Place*—was published by Mayapple Press in 2008. She teaches poetry to kids in area schools and to adults through the University of Chicago's Graham School. Her essay on collaboration with Cecilia Pinto is forthcoming in the anthology *Mentor and Muse* (SIU Press, 2010). Her backyard garden in Evanston this year will bloom, and bloom. The Shasta daisies will not droop.

Reginald Gibbons is the author of nine books of poems—most recently *Creatures of a Day* and *Slow Trains Overhead: Chicago Poems and Stories*—and two chapbooks. He has also published a novel, *Sweetbitter*, and other works, including translations of Sophocles, Euripides, and Mexican and Spanish poets. He is a co-founder of The Guild Literary Complex, the former editor of *TriQuarterly* magazine (1981-97), the founder of the graduate creative writing program at Northwestern, and a longtime resident of Chicago. He teaches at Northwestern University, and lives in Evanston with his wife, the writer Cornelia Spelman.

Chris Green is the author of two books of poetry: *Epiphany School* and *The Sky Over Walgreens*. His poetry has appeared in such journals as *Poetry*, *Verse*, *Black Clock*, and *North American Review*. He edited the anthology, *A Writers' Congress: Chicago Poets on Barack Obama's Inauguration*. He teaches poetry at DePaul University and is a Visiting Fellow at DePaul's Humanities Center.

Arielle Greenberg is the co-author, with Rachel Zucker, of *Home/Birth: A Poemic* (1913 Press, forthcoming 2011), and author of *My Kafka Century* (Action Books, 2005), *Given* (Verse, 2002) and the chapbooks *Shake Her* (Dusie Kollektiv, 2009) and *Farther Down: Songs from the Allergy Trials* (New Michigan, 2003). She is co-editor of three anthologies: with Rachel Zucker, *Starting Today: 100 Poems for Obama's First 100 Days* (Iowa, 2010) and *Women*

Poets on Mentorship: Efforts and Affections (Iowa, 2008); and with Lara Glenum, *Gurlesque* (Saturnalia, 2010). Twice featured in *Best American Poetry* and the recipient of a MacDowell Colony fellowship, she is the founder-moderator of the poet-moms listserv and is an Associate Professor at Columbia College Chicago.

Susan Hahn is the author of eight books of poetry and two produced plays with a third one advancing at a major theater in Chicago. She just completed her first novel. Among her awards for writing is a Guggenheim Fellowship.

Miles Harvey is the author of *Painter in a Savage Land: The Strange Saga of the First European Artist in North America* (Random House, 2008), which received a 2008 Editors' Choice award from *Booklist* and a best-books citation from *The Chicago Tribune*. His previous book, *The Island of Lost Maps: A True Story of Cartographic Crime* (Random House), a national and international bestseller, was selected by *USA Today* as one of the ten best books of 2000. The recipient of a 2007-2008 Knight-Wallace fellowship at the University of Michigan and a 2004-2005 Illinois Arts Council Award for fiction, Harvey has taught at Northwestern University, the University of Chicago and the University of New Orleans. He recently joined the faculty at DePaul University in Chicago.

Mary Hawley is the author of *Double Tongues* and co-translator of the bilingual poetry anthology *Astillas de luz/Shards of Light,* both published by Tía Chucha Press. She has been active in the Chicago poetry community for many years, and her poems have appeared in various journals and anthologies, including *Notre Dame Review, The Bloomsbury Review, Hawaii Pacific Review, Spoon River Poetry Review, Another Chicago Magazine,* and *Power Lines: A Decade of Poetry from Chicago's Guild Complex.*

Liam Heneghan is an ecosystem ecologist working at DePaul University where he is a Professor of Environmental Science and co-director of DePaul University's Institute for Nature and Culture. His research has included studies on the impact of acid rain on soil foodwebs in Europe, and on interbiome comparisons of decomposition and nutrient dynamics in forested ecosystems in North American and in the tropics. Over the past decade Heneghan and his students have been working on restoration issues in Midwestern ecosystems. Heneghan is co-chair of the Chicago Wilderness Science Team. He is also a graduate student in philosophy, a part-time model, and an occasional poet.

Edward Hirsch, a Chicago native and MacArthur Fellow, has just published *The Living Fire: New and Selected Poems*, which brings together thirty-five years of poetry from seven previous collections, including *For the Sleepwalkers* (1981), *Wild Gratitude* (1986), which won the National Book Critics Circle Award, *The Night Parade* (1989), *Earthly Measures* (1994), *On Love* (1998), *Lay Back the Darkness* (2003), and *Special Orders* (2008). He has also written four prose books, including *How to Read a Poem and Fall in Love with Poetry* (1999), a national bestseller, and *Poet's Choice* (2006). He edits the series "The Writer's World" (Trinity University Press). He has edited Theodore Roethke's *Selected Poems* (2005) and co-edited *The Making of a Sonnet: A Norton Anthology* (2008). He has received a Guggenheim Fellowship and the American Academy of Arts and Letters Award for Literature. He taught in the Creative Writing Program at the University of Houston for seventeen years and now serves as president of the John Simon Guggenheim Memorial Foundation.

Randall Honold is an administrator and adjunct faculty member at DePaul University. At this point in time he likes India, bicycles, cameras, a variety of bands whose members are half his age, and speculative fiction about environmentally stressed urbanity. He continues to love his family and shall forever.

Susen James lives in the concrete & steel shadow of Chicago. She writes poetry to remain sane. She teaches Poetry & Fantasy Literature at Columbia College.

Rachel Jamison Webster is an Artist-in-Residence in Poetry at Northwestern University. She won and Academy of American Poets Young Poets Prize and was recently honored by the Poetry Center of Chicago and the Poetry Foundation as an outstanding emerging artist. Her poems have appeared in many journals, including *Poetry*, *The Southern Review*, *Blackbird* and *Redivider*. A chapbook, *The Blue Grotto*, was published by Dancing Girl Press in 2009. She edits the online anthology of international poetry, UniVerse, located at www.universeofpoetry.org. More of Rachel's writing can be read at www.//racheljamisonwebster.blogspot.com.

Larry Janowski's most recent book is *BrotherKeeper* (The Puddin'head Press 2007). He is a 2008 recipient of an Illinois Arts Council Literary Award and a contributor to *A Writers' Congress: Chicago Poets on Barack Obama's Inauguration* (DePaul Poetry Institute 2009). Larry is a Franciscan friar and teaches poetry at Loyola University.

Allan Johnston's poems have been published in *Poetry*, *Poetry East*, *Rhino*, and over sixty other journals. He is the author of one poetry collection (*Tasks of Survival*) and a recipient of an Illinois Arts Council Fellowship and a Pushcart Prize nomination. Originally from California, he earned his M.A. in Creative Writing and his Ph.D. in English from the University of California, Davis, and now teaches writing and literature at Columbia College and DePaul University in Chicago. He currently serves as a reader for the Illinois Emerging Poets competition and is president of the Society for the Philosophical Study of Education. In the past he has worked as a sheepherder, shakesplitter, roofer, forest fire fighter, Indian cook, and photographer, among other occupations.

Richard Jones is the author of several books of poetry, including *Apropos of Nothing* and *The Correct Spelling & Exact Meaning*.

Peter Karklins is a Chicago artist.

Kathleen Kirk is the author of *Selected Roles* (Moon Journal Press, 2006), *Broken Sonnets* (Finishing Line Press, 2009), and *Living on the Earth* (Finishing Line, 2010, New Women's Voices Series, No. 74). Her poems, stories, and essays appear in a variety of print and online journals, including *Apparatus, Common Review, Ekphrasis, Fourth River, Greensboro Review, Ninth Letter, Poems & Plays,* and *Spoon River Poetry Review*. Her poem "The Bright Day" is included in *A Writers' Congress: Chicago Poets on Barack Obama's Inauguration*, edited by Chris Green, and published by The DePaul Poetry Institute, DePaul Humanities Center in 2009.

Sean D. Kirkland is an Assistant Professor in the Department of Philosophy at DePaul University. He has published primarily in the areas of ancient Greek philosophy and literature, but on contemporary continental thought as well. His book, *The Ontology of Socratic Questioning in Plato's Early Dialogues*, should be out soon with SUNY Press.

Billy Lombardo is the author of three books of fiction, (*The Man with Two Arms, How to Hold a Woman,* and *The Logic of a Rose: Chicago Stories*) and a book of poetry/prose, (*Meanwhile, Roxy Mourns*). He is the co-founder and artistic director of *Polyphony H.S.*, a nonprofit, national student-run literary magazine for high school writers and editors. He holds an MFA in Creative Writing from Warren Wilson College. He teaches English literature and creative writing at the Latin School of Chicago and teaches fiction for UCLA's Extension program. He lives in Forest Park, Illinois, thirteen miles from 35th and Shields, where the White Sox play ball.

Patricia McMillen is an Illinois journalist, musician, and death penalty abolitionist. She has received numerous awards and honors, including an Illinois Arts Council poetry fellowship (2002), and earned a Masters Degree in English from the University of Illinois Chicago Program for Writers (2005). Her poems have appeared in many literary journals and in two anthologies. In 2006, her first poetry chapbook, *Knife Lake Anthology*—a collection of seventeen poems depicting the social milieu and costs of capital punishment—was published by Puddinghouse Publications (Columbus, OH). Her full-length poetry collection, *Losing It*, is seeking a publisher.

E. Ethelbert Miller is a literary activist. He is the board chair of the Institute for Policy Studies, a progressive think tank located in Washington, D.C. He is also the director of the African American Resource Center at Howard University. The author of several collections of poetry, he has also written two memoirs, *Fathering Words: The Making of an African American Writer* (2000) and *The 5TH Inning* (2009). Mr. Miller is often heard on National Public Radio.

Ralph J. Mills, Jr. (1931–2007) Born in Chicago, Ralph J. Mills, Jr. lived nearly his entire life in the city. He was the author of numerous critical monographs, three volumes of essays and thirteen books of poetry. He was the editor of Theodore Roethke's prose and letters and of *The Notebooks of David Ignatow*. His poetry collection, *Living With Distance* (1979), received the Society of Midland Authors prize for poetry, and *March Light* was awarded the Carl Sandburg Award. His last book of poems, *Grasses Standing: Selected Poems* (2000) was awarded the William Carlos Williams Prize from the Poetry Society of America. *Essays on Poetry,* a compilation of his criticism, was published in 2003. He taught first at the University of Chicago where he was Associate Chairman of the Committee on Social Thought, then at the University of Illinois at Chicago where he was professor of literature, poetry, and creative writing for over thirty years. (The editors are grateful to Ralph's daughter, Natalie, for her assistance.)

Patricia Monaghan is Professor of Interdisciplinary Studies at DePaul University's School for New Learning. She is the author of four books of poetry, most recently the extended meditation on the impact of war on families, *Homefront*, and has won a Pushcart Prize as well as the Friends of Literature Award for poetry. She is Senior Fellow at the Black Earth Institute, a progressive think-tank for artists.

Michele Morano is the author of the travel memoir, *Grammar Lessons: Translating a Life in Spain*. Her creative work has appeared in anthologies and literary journals such as *Best American Essays*, *Fourth Genre*, *Georgia Review*, and *Missouri Review*. She is associate professor of English at DePaul University.

Deborah Nodler Rosen edits *RHINO*, an award-winning poetry journal, and serves on the Board of UniVerse of Poetry. Her anthology, *WHERE WE FIND OURSELVES: Jewish Women around the World Write about Home*, was recently published by SUNY Press. Her poems have been published in *Third Coast; Out of Line; New Poetry Appreciation,* Kunming, China; *THE JOURNAL*, Northwestern School of Continuing Studies; *Where We Live-Illinois Poets;* and elsewhere. Prizes include First Prize in both an Oregon State Poetry Association Contest and California State Poetry Society Contest. Rosen leads poetry workshops and teaches poetry in schools under a KIDS MEET ART program.

Julie Parson Nesbitt is author of the poetry collection *Finders* (West End Press). She received the Gwendolyn Brooks "Significant Illinois Poet" Award and holds an MFA in Creative Writing from the University of Pittsburgh. Her poetry has been published in numerous anthologies. One of the first Chicago poets to be featured in the Poetry Slams and to open Chicago bars to poetry readings, she served as executive director of the Guild Complex, a cross-cultural literary arts center, where she presented more than 100 literary events annually and was Director of Development for Young Chicago Authors, which presents Louder Than A Bomb, the world's largest annual teen poetry festival.

Elise Paschen is the author of *Bestiary* (Red Hen Press, 2009), *Infidelities*, winner of the Nicholas Roerich Poetry Prize, and *Houses: Coasts*. Her poems have been published in numerous anthologies and magazines, including *The New Republic, The Hudson Review*, and *TriQuarterly*. She is the editor of *The New York Times* best-selling anthology *Poetry Speaks to Children* and *Poetry*

Speaks Who I Am and co-editor of *Poetry Speaks, Poetry Speaks Expanded, Poetry in Motion,* and *Poetry in Motion from Coast to Coast*. Former Executive Director of the Poetry Society of America, Paschen teaches in the Writing Program at the School of the Art Institute of Chicago.

Cecilia Pinto is a writer who has made her home in Chicago for over twenty years. She is currently the director of the Hands on Stanzas program for The Poetry Center of Chicago. Her work has appeared in *Fence, Diagram, Rhino, Quarter After Eight* and elsewhere.

Christina Pugh is the author of two books of poems: *Restoration* (TriQuarterly Books / Northwestern University Press, 2008) and *Rotary* (Word Press, 2004; winner of the Word Press First Book Prize), as well as the chapbook *Gardening at Dusk* (Wells College Press, 2002). Her poems have also appeared in *The Atlantic Monthly, Poetry, TriQuarterly,* and other publications. Her honors have included the Lucille Medwick Memorial Award from the Poetry Society of America, an individual artist fellowship in poetry from the Illinois Arts Council, and the Grolier Poetry Prize. She is an associate professor of English at the University of Illinois at Chicago.

Mike Puican has had his poetry published in journals such as: *Michigan Quarterly Review, New England Review, Another Chicago Magazine, The Bloomsbury Review, Third Coast Review, Parthenon West* and *Malahat Review.* He won the 2004 Tia Chucha Press Chapbook Contest for his chapbook, *30 Seconds.* Mike was a member of the 1996 Chicago Slam Team. He recently completed an MFA in Poetry at Warren Wilson College.

Ed Roberson is author of eight books of poetry. His most recent book, *The New Wing of the Labyrinth* was published by Singing Horse Press in 2009. *City Eclogue,* was published spring 2006, Number 23 in the Atelos series. His collection, *Voices Cast Out to Talk Us In,* was a winner of the Iowa Poetry Prize; his book *Atmosphere Condition* was a winner of the National Poetry Series and was nominated for the Academy of American Poets' Lenore

Marshall Award. He is a recipient of the Lila Wallace Writers' Award and the Poetry Society of America's Shelley Memorial Award. His next book, *To See the Earth Before the End of the World*, is due out from Wesleyan University Press in the fall of 2010. He is currently Artist in Residence at Northwestern University teaching in the English Department, Creative Writing Program.

cin salach has collaborated with musicians, video artists, dancers and photographers for over 20 years in such groups as The Loofah Method, Betty's Mouth and ten tongues. Her first book, *Looking for a Soft Place to Land,* was published by Tia Chucha Press. She has been widely published in journals and anthologies, most recently, *Starting Today: 100 Poems for Obama's First 100 Days*, Iowa Press. An Illinois Arts Council recipient and four-time Ragdale fellow, cin is also co-founder of Words@Play, a collaboration with the Chicago Park District and the Children's Humanities Festival. More rural than urban, she lives by the Ravenswood train tracks but secretly pretends it's a river.

Maureen Seaton's recent publications include *Cave of the Yellow Volkswagen* (Carnegie Mellon University Press, 2009); *America Loves Carney* (Sow's Ear, 2009); and *Sex Talks to Girls: A Memoir* (University of Wisconsin Press Living Out Series, 2008), winner of the Lambda Literary Award. The recipient of an NEA and two Pushcarts, she currently teaches poetry, literary collage, and collaboration at the University of Miami.

Don Share is Senior Editor of *Poetry* magazine in Chicago. His books include *Squandermania* (Salt Publishing), *Union* (Zoo Press), *The Traumatophile* (Scantily Clad Press), and *Seneca in English* (Penguin Classics); forthcoming are *Bunting's Persia* (Flood Editions), and a critical edition of Basil Bunting's poems (Faber and Faber). His translations of Miguel Hernández, collected in *I Have Lots of Heart* (Bloodaxe Books) were awarded the *Times Literary Supplement* Translation Prize, the Premio Valle Inclán Prize, and the PEN/New England Discovery Award. He has been Poetry Editor of *Harvard Review* and *Partisan Review*, Editor *of Literary Imagination*, and Curator of Poetry at Harvard University.

James Shea is the author of *Star in the Eye*, selected for the 2008 Fence Modern Poets Series. His poems have appeared in various journals, including *American Letters and Commentary*, *Boston Review*, *Colorado Review*, *jubilat*, and *Verse*. He is currently an Assistant Professor at Nebraska Wesleyan University.

Barry Silesky authored three books of poems and biographies of Ferlinghetti and John Gardner; poems and non-fiction in many magazines—*Tampa Review*, *Notre Dame Review*, *Missouri Review*, et al.

Marc Smith is the creator and founder of the International Poetry Slam movement. As stated in the PBS television series, *The United States of Poetry*, a "strand of new poetry began at Chicago's Green Mill Tavern in 1987 when Marc Smith found a home for the Poetry Slam." He has performed at the Kennedy Center, the Smithsonian Institute, Galway's Cruit Festival, Denmark's Roskilde Festival, Ausburg's ABC Brecht Festival, and the Queensland Poetry Fest in Australia. He has hosted over 1000 standing room only shows at the Green Mill's original slam and has been featured on CNN, 60 Minutes, and National Public Radio. He narrated the Sourcebooks releases *Spoken Word Revolution* and *Spoken Word Revolution Redux*. Marc's volume of poetry *Crowdpleaser* (Collage Press) and his CDs *It's About Time, Quarters in the Juke Box,* and *Love & Politics* are available through his website www.slampapi.com.

Patricia Smith is the author of five books of poetry, including *Blood Dazzler*, a finalist for the 2008 National Book Award, and *Teahouse of the Almighty*, a National Poetry Series selection. She also authored the ground-breaking history *Africans in America* and the award-winning children's book *Janna and the Kings*. Her work has appeared in *Poetry*, *The Paris Review*, *TriQuarterly* and many other journals, and she has been performed around the world, including Carnegie Hall and the Poets Stage in Stockholm. She is a Pushcart Prize winner and a four-time individual champion of the National Poetry

Slam, the most successful poet in the competition's history. A professor at the City University of New York/College of Staten Island, she also serves on the faculty of Cave Canem and the Stonecoast MFA program at the University of Southern Maine.

Maureen Tolman Flannery's most recent book of poems about Latin America is *Destiny Whispers to the Beloved*. Other volumes of her work include *Ancestors in the Landscape, Secret of the Rising up, A Fine Line* and *Knowing Stones*. Maureen and her actor husband Dan have raised their four children in Chicago. She now works at the Chicago Waldorf School where they were educated. Her poems have appeared in fifty anthologies and over a hundred literary reviews, including *Birmingham Poetry Review, Xavier Review, Calyx, Pedestal, Atlanta Review, Out of Line,* and *North American Review, Poetry East,* and *Santa Fe Literary Review*.

Tony Trigilio's books include the poetry collection *The Lama's English Lessons* (Three Candles Press, 2006), and the chapbooks *With the Memory, Which is Enormous* (Main Street Rag, 2009) and *Make a Joke and I Will Sigh and You Will Laugh and I Will Cry* (e-chap, Scantily Clad Press, 2008). With Tim Prchal, he edited *Visions and Divisions: American Immigration Literature, 1870-1930* (Rutgers University Press, 2008). He teaches at Columbia College Chicago, and is a co-founder and co-editor of *Court Green*.

David Trinidad's most recent books are *The Late Show* (2007) and *By Myself* (with D.A. Powell, 2009), both published by Turtle Point Press. *Dear Prudence: New and Selected Poems* is forthcoming from Turtle Point in fall 2011. He teaches poetry at Columbia College Chicago, where he co-edits the journal *Court Green*.

Mark Turcotte is the author of the poetry collections *The Feathered Heart* and *Exploding Chippewas*. He lives in Chicago, where he serves as Visiting Assistant Professor in English at DePaul University.

Martha Modena Vertreace-Doody, a National Endowment for the Arts Fellow, is Distinguished Professor of English and Poet-in-Residence at Kennedy-King College, Chicago, IL. She received her MFA at Vermont College. Her books include *Second House from the Corner*, *Under a Cat's-Eye Moon*, *Oracle Bones*, *Cinnabar*, *Smokeless Flame*, *Kelly in the Mirror*, *Maafa: When Night Becomes a Lion*, *Dragon Lady:Tsukimi*, and *Glacier Fire*. She has poems in *Illinois Voices: An Anthology of Twentieth-Century Poetry* (University of Illinois Press, 2001) and *Poets of the New Century* (David R. Godine Publisher, 2001). Illinois Poet Laureate Kevin Stein published her poem "Walking Under Night Sky" in his cassette *Bread & Steel: Illlinois Poets Reading from Their Works*. She lives in Chicago with her husband, Tim, and their cats, Fred and Patrick Samuel.

Dolores Wilber received her M.F.A. from The School of the Art Institute and has operated her own graphic design and multidisciplinary art practice for over twenty years. Her multidisciplinary approach embraces cross-pollination between design and art in print, installation, video, performance and radio. Her work has been exhibited widely including in Chicago, Cleveland, Ann Arbor, London, Estonia, Portugal, Germany, and China. She has received many awards including Illinois Arts Council Fellowships, an American Embassy Travel grant, and a Peabody Award for her work for the national public radio program This American Life. Her short film, *Chests*, was premiered at the Ann Arbor Film Festival. She has taught at DePaul since 1997 and was named Professor in 2010.

Barbara Willard, Ph.D. is an Associate Professor in the College of Communication at DePaul University. Her research involves the rhetoric of landscapes as they are both read by and created by humans. Additionally, she examines how the rhetoric of popular culture and environmental rhetoric intersect, informing and influencing cultural practice. She also conducts research that assists in the development of public campaigns that fosters sustainable behavior such as natural landscaping and support for restoration practices. She has published in a variety of academic journals including *Environmental Communication*, *Rhetoric Society Quarterly* and the *Journal of Popular Culture*.

Christian Wiman's latest book of poetry, *Every Riven Thing*, was published by Farrar, Straus and Giroux in November, 2010. He is the editor of *Poetry*.

S.L. Wisenberg is an award-winning writer of fiction, nonfiction and poetry. She's published a story collection, *The Sweetheart Is In*; an essay collection, *Holocaust Girls: History, Memory & Other Obsessions*; and a nonfiction chronicle, *The Adventures of Cancer Bitch*. She co-directs the MA/MFA in Creative Writing program at Northwestern University.

Perry A. Zurn is a PhD candidate in philosophy at DePaul University. Having previously studied the history of philosophy at Oxford, Villanova, and Miami University, Zurn is interested in applying the relatively new disciplines of post-structuralism and psycho-analysis to the age old questions of nature, religion, and translation.